MONITORING & EVALUATION
made easy

A HANDBOOK FOR
VOLUNTARY ORGANISATIONS

ANNE CONNOR

EDINBURGH   HMSO

ISBN 0 11 494229 3

Acknowledgements

I wish to thank all the people – staff, volunteers, managers and users – in NCH, Age Concern Scotland and the day care centres who gave so generously of their enthusiasm, ideas and time in the field work on which this report and handbook are based.

I also wish to acknowledge the co-operation of staff in Social Work, Community Education and other local authority Departments, Health Boards and other agencies throughout Scotland, in explaining their information needs and experiences in working with voluntary organisations.

Thanks are also due to colleagues and friends within The Scottish Office, voluntary organisations, research units and other settings who gave invaluable feedback, advice and encouragement. I am especially grateful to Bill Bennett, with whom I developed the original concept and who has been unfaltering in his good sense and support throughout.

FOREWORD: HOW TO USE THIS HANDBOOK

This handbook has been prepared for people in voluntary organisations who want to describe, review and plan their activities. The book is not meant to be read through and then left on the shelf. It is meant to be used as part of your day-to-day work in managing or carrying out the activities of your voluntary organisation. It should be dipped into and referred to for ideas as well as for solutions to problems. Make friends with it. Write notes in the margins and put sticky labels at the parts you are using now and at bits you want to come back to later. This is also a book which should be read afresh from time to time: as organisations and the people within them develop and change, so the ways their activities are described and assessed need to change with them.

Even if you have done this sort of work before, the first part which explains what monitoring and evaluation are all about is a good starting point. Where you go from there depends on your current circumstances.

If you are starting off a new project or new activity and want to establish information systems from the outset, or if you want to rethink your existing arrangements – for example, see if they could be made a bit easier – then take some time over the section on "Getting Started".

The rest of the large middle part is about putting monitoring and evaluation into practice. For projects which are starting from scratch, the next section on finding out who uses the project is the logical place to begin.

If your project is already underway and you have a particular information problem – and you know what this is – then you can go straight to the appropriate section on user feedback or whatever. There is a short introduction which will help you check if this is what you are after and narrow down the best approach to your problem. If you know exactly what you are after just look up the right Case Example: there is a detailed list in the contents pages and a chart which notes when a particular approach tackles two types of problems.

If you are less certain what particular aspects you need to be looking at, read through the introductory part of each section in Part 2. You might also find it useful to skim through the case examples: several of these refer readers to other case examples in the handbooks which tackle related problems.

If, however, you already have all your information to hand but are struggling to get it into order, or have to produce a report for your funder by next week, go straight to Part 3. Once the panic is over you can peruse the rest of the handbook at your leisure and pick up a few tips on how to avoid the last minute rush next year.

Management committees and funders will probably want to look at Parts 1 and 3. This will be useful when planning your own arrangements and considering how to make monitoring and evaluation by project staff as productive as possible. Once you want to get into the details of particular aspects, or want to look at some of the ideas from people working in real settings, the rest of the handbook can be dipped into as needed.

The time that I spent with the voluntary organisations while preparing this handbook and doing the research on which it is based was good fun as well as hard work. I hope the monitoring and evaluation you do with this handbook is as enjoyable.

Anne Connor

MONITORING AND EVALUATION MADE EASY

A HANDBOOK FOR VOLUNTARY ORGANISATIONS

Annex

MONITORING AND EVALUATION ISSUS ADDRESSED BY TOOLS

COVERED BY THE CASE EXAMPLES

CASE EXAMPLES	SCALE AND PATTERN OF USE	CHARACTERISTICS OF USERS	OUTCOMES	USERS' VIEWS	AGENCIES' VIEWS	ORGANISATION	FEASABILITY
CE 3	X	X					
CE 4	X						
CE 5	X						
CE 6	X						
CE 7		X	X				
CE 8	X		X				
CE 9				X			
CE 10			X	X			
CE 11				X			
CE 12				X			
CE 13				X			
CE 14					X		
CE 15			X		X		
CE 16						X	
CE 17						X	
CE 18						X	
CE 19							X
CE 20							X

PART ONE:
WHAT THIS IS ALL ABOUT

1

Introduction

NEED FOR MONITORING AND EVALUATION

More than ever before voluntary organisations need reliable information about their activities. They also need to be able to assess their progress and plan for the future in a more vigorous, objective way than before.

There are two broad reasons why any activity or service should be looked at in this way: to provide the best service possible for the people who use it and to demonstrate its value and achievements to other people.

Providing the best service to users entails:

- listening to users' views;
- considering how the circumstances of people who use the service are changing and whether the service should also change;
- reviewing the response given to individual people and ensuring it reflects their needs;
- feeding back to and liaising with other service providers;
- thinking about people in the target group who do not use the service and how their needs can be met;
- checking that the best use is made of available resources – people's time and skills, physical space, equipment and money;
- ensuring that paid and volunteer staff know what they are achieving and are aware of the outcomes for users.

Demonstrating the achievements of a service or organisation involves:

- drawing it to the attention of people who may want to use it or who have some other interest;

- reassuring users, their families and other professionals about the quality of our work;
- letting other people learn from our achievements and disappointments, especially when it is an innovative or unusual enterprise;
- accountability to those who fund or assist the project or organisation – whether they are the public, organisations giving help-in-kind or major public sector or other funders.

Voluntary organisations need good information about their activities for their own purposes. Knowing how your service is being used and what users think of it will be useful in many situations, for example:

- targetting information about your service where it can best reach the people who use – or do not yet use – the project;
- day-to-day planning, such as knowing when the busy times are, when more volunteer or paid workers are needed;
- management matters, such as arranging training to take account of changing demands on the service;
- identifying problems early on so they can be tackled before they become too difficult or badly affect users;
- longer-term planning for the project – which parts should be developed and in what ways.

Many local authorities, central government and other funders have been reviewing their requirements for information from recipient voluntary organisations. This has been prompted by 2 developments.

The new community care arrangements, which are expected to lead to an increased role for voluntary organisations providing direct care services. All groups receiving funds from Social Work Departments (Social Services Departments in England and Wales) will need to keep more detailed records on the number of people using services, get feedback from users and hold regular reviews of cases to ensure each person is still benefiting from the service.

The review of Government funding to the voluntary sector, which has required all Government funding schemes to ensure recipient voluntary organisations continue to meet their objectives and are sensitive to the views of and outcomes for users.

Many other funders – such as other local authority departments, health boards and Trusts – agree with the ideas and good practice promoted in these documents and have been reviewing their arrangements along broadly similar lines.

THE RESEARCH STUDY

Given these new expectations on voluntary organisations, the Social Work Services Group of The Scottish Office carried out a research study to establish how far groups could carry out reliable monitoring and evaluation of their own activities. A researcher worked with 26 voluntary projects providing direct care to older people, children and families. These included large and well-established organisations as well as smaller and newer groups located throughout Scotland. The views and experiences of other local projects and of local authorities and other funders were also considered.

The study found that it was possible for voluntary organisations in various circumstances to monitor and evaluate their work in a way that met their information needs and those of other people such as funders. However this was more likely to happen and was easier if certain factors applied.

• **The organisation must be clear what they are measuring their achievements against.** This means the project has to have clear aims and objectives, stated in terms that are achievable and measurable. Other organisations with whom the project works must also be clear about the expectations they have of the project.

• **Both the project and the other people concerned have to be realistic about what can be done.** It is necessary to take account of:

  ° the other demands that are on the project, especially the delivery of direct services for which it exists;

  ° the input from staff and volunteers and the skills and knowledge which they bring to the monitoring and evaluation tasks;

  ° time needed to undertake this work;

  ° the type of services that are being provided and any inherent technical difficulties in monitoring and evaluation which are associated with these; and

  ° the existing level of information gathering.

Not all organisations are starting from the same place and they cannot be expected to maintain the same level of progress.

* The voluntary project needs to have good, accessible management support.
This is needed to give impetus and on-going direction and support to the
monitoring and evaluation work, to help the project maintain the appropriate
balance between delivering services and monitoring and evaluating these
activities, and then to address the issues which the monitoring and evaluation
findings will identify for the project and perhaps the wider organisation.

• The people concerned must believe that these tasks are worthwhile. This
especially applies to the staff who have to carry out the burden of the monitoring
and evaluation work. They should be able to have confidence that the
appropriate people will listen and take account of the findings and that there is
scope for positive changes to be made if these are found to be needed.

A summary of the full report is included as an Annex to this handbook. The experience of the participating projects and findings from this study are described in detail in "Monitoring and Evaluation by Voluntary Organisations: Research Report". A booklet on monitoring and evaluation by day care centres for older people – "Tell Them All About It" – has also been published by Age Concern Scotland.

HANDBOOK ON MONITORING AND EVALUATION

In addition to the main reports, the practical experience of the fieldwork has been brought together in this handbook. This shows the methods of obtaining feedback from users, of establishing the scale of use of the service and other techniques developed by the projects. It also demonstrates practical ways of tackling the difficulties identified in the study for the voluntary projects themselves or for other people such as managers and funders.

Purpose of the Handbook

The intention is that this guide will be used by voluntary organisations to help them describe, review and plan their own activities. The examples given in the handbook are only starting points: they will probably need to be adapted to suit each project's own particular circumstances.

The examples are drawn from the fieldwork and so are mainly based on projects working with older people or children and families. However the application of these ideas and experiences is not limited to these settings: the way in which an advice centre for homeless young adults records who uses the service and what users think of it is relevant to most advice services. By the same token, although a method is suggested for a particular type of service here this may not be relevant to every similar project. The type of information problem – what it is the project wants to find out – is the most important factor in deciding what method is right in their circumstances.

This research study was based on the needs of and challenges facing voluntary organisations providing direct social care services. The kind of problems which these projects faced are often experienced by workers in statutory settings, and it is hoped that they may also be able to get ideas from and adapt the approaches suggested here. Similarly, voluntary organisations undertaking different activities – for example, on environmental or community development projects – may find parallels to their situations. Voluntary organisations which undertake an intermediary role in supporting and co-ordinating the activities of other voluntary organisations have different information needs which have not been tested by this research study. For them, the relevance of this handbook may lie in the underlying approach – in identifying the information needs of the organisation from the bottom up, addressing the consequences for and demands on managers and making good, systematic monitoring and evaluation an integral part of the organisation's work.

Layout of the Handbook

The rest of the first part of the handbook explains what monitoring and evaluation mean and how they relate to other aspects of day to day management and planning for the future. It also considers ways of setting indicators or measurements for the quality of services.

The second part of the guide has 7 sections:

- planning for monitoring and evaluation by the project;
- establishing how people use the service – the scale and pattern of use;
- identifying what changes have occurred, especially the outcomes for users;
- getting feedback from individual users;
- obtaining feedback from agencies;
- looking at aspects of the way the project is organised; and
- checking the feasibility of new services.

Each section has an introductory part which explains the circumstances in which this arose in the research study and more general issues associated with this aspect of collecting and using information. This is followed by a few Case Examples, showing how projects in the fieldwork tackled particular aspects or used the approach in different circumstances. Copies of any relevant forms or questionnaires are given at the end of each example.

Part 3 of the handbook covers matters that might be useful to voluntary organisations gathering information on any of these matters. A checklist of points of information which the research study found that most funders want voluntary organisations to provide is given in the first section.

A list of steps which project staff, managers and funders could each take to make monitoring and evaluation by voluntary organisations easier and more effective was also drawn from the research findings, and this is included at Section 2. Again, this complements the suggestions given in specific Case Examples in Part 2.

Some funders tell their recipient organisations what is needed in their circumstances, but groups may find it useful to refer to this more general checklist when thinking about the information they need. In the same way, some funders give useful guidance on how they would like voluntary organisations to present information about their achievements in annual reports or other forms of feedback. However, not every agency gives this type of advice and many staff and managers of voluntary organisations find this matter particularly difficult. A short section on preparing reports has been included at Section 3. There is also a section on how to analyse information, especially if you do not have a computer, and how to present your findings in tables.

Finally, people using this handbook may want more advice and ideas, or may wish to read further about monitoring and evaluation. A list of useful contacts and publications is given at Section 5 of Part 3.

B

2

Monitoring and Evaluation

WHAT MONITORING AND EVALUATION ARE

The words 'monitoring' and 'evaluation', along with other phrases such as 'quality assurance', 'performance indicators' and 'value for money' used to be heard only in relation to business. Now they are also being used more often in connection with other forms of activity such as education and social care services. On the face of it, many voluntary organisations might feel that all of this has little to do with them, and that their services and activities cannot be described and measured in these ways. However the reality is that staff and managers in voluntary organisations, like most people, have already been doing these tasks for a long time. What has changed are the ways we describe them and the fact that these tasks are now being done more consciously than before.

> *Monitoring* is the on-going checking of progress against a plan through routine, systematic collection and review of information. It is concerned with noticing differences over time and with providing a regular check on what we are doing against what we are supposed to be doing.

- Is the number of people coming to our centre more or less than at the same time last year?
- How much have we spent so far this year, and is this in line with our estimated budget?

Monitoring is essentially value free. It does not set out to tell us whether an increase or decrease in the number of users is particularly good or bad. It also does not address the question of whether these are the kind of activities we should be offering users in the first place.

> *Evaluation,* on the other hand, is concerned with making an assessment. This is judging the merit of an activity or plan and measuring it against specific criteria. It is concerned with an assessment of the effects or outcomes of an activity, and compares these with the goals which the activity was intended to achieve.

- How well are we meeting the needs of our users?

- Are people more aware than before about the environment (or their welfare rights, or whatever)?

- Have we made the best use of our resources, or would another approach let as achieve more?

Evaluation is also concerned with understanding why things have worked out in the way that they have, and with learning from achievements and disappointments. As such, it is often a specific, occasional activity – a "stop and think".

Evaluation can also take account of other criteria which have not been specified in the aims. For example, most local authorities and voluntary organisations have a policy of equality of access to all potential users, irrespective of gender, race, disability or other characteristics. Even if this were not mentioned, however, a voluntary organisation or funder might still take special account of whether a project's activities and the way these were organised met good practice standards on equal opportunities. Similarly, whether a project is making sensible use of its resources can be expected to be a factor in any evaluation of its progress and achievements.

Monitoring and evaluation are closely linked to each other, since the information gained from the monitoring will play a large part in any evaluation. In the same way, neither monitoring nor evaluation are an end in themselves. Both of these are preceded by setting up the initial aims and goals and then planning how these can be put into effect. They are then followed by revising our activities and aims and making any necessary changes. This is sometimes referred to as a "planning cycle" and the diagram below shows how these various stages relate to each other.

Planning Cycle

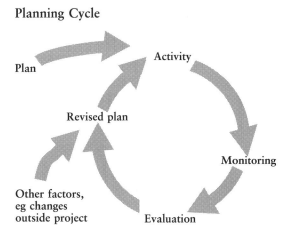

These are intellectual activities which we do every day, both inside and outside a work setting. For example, when planning where to go on holiday we decide what our requirements are (setting the aims and objectives) and perhaps which are the most important among these (prioritising the criteria) – hot weather? somewhere not too expensive? a beach? Once we are there we keep an eye on the weather and how the money is lasting and perhaps make some adjustments to take account of these (monitoring). Next year we can think back over our previous experience – did it achieve what we wanted? what would we do differently? We might want to rethink our criteria – maybe we really want somewhere a bit cooler or quieter (evaluation, leading to a revised plan or the decision to retain the original criteria and aims).

The points which monitoring and evaluation take account of will depend on the circumstances of the project or activity concerned and what people carrying out the monitoring and evaluation tasks consider important. On the example of the holiday, it is quite common for two people who have been away together to give rather different accounts of whether they enjoyed it. The experience was the same, but their expectations or what it was that they considered most important – the criteria – have been different. In the same way, a project and its funder can have different criteria and so come to different conclusions about the success of a service or activity. For example, a centre for unemployed workers might consider users feeling more confident and taking on more active roles in local affairs as the most important achievement, while someone else might judge it by the number of people gaining employment.

The focus in this handbook and research study is on monitoring and evaluation by projects of their own activities. It is therefore concerned with reflecting the aspects which they think are important. Other people, such as those funding the services or referring users to them, will have their own interests. The voluntary organisation can check this with the other agencies and plan to cover points of information they want to know. Alternatively, the project can expect the other agencies to do their own evaluations, often drawing on the same basic information from the monitoring element.

In any consideration of what and how a project is doing, it is important to keep in mind whether you are concerned with the level of activity or with the outcomes of the activity or with both, as is usually the case.

Efficiency is about the level of activity. This is defined as the relationship between the inputs (staff and volunteer time, buildings, money etc) and the outputs (number of people seen etc). An example might be the work of two housing advice centres, one based in the town centre with a higher rent and paying for extra staff and volunteers, while the other is in a housing estate and costs half as much to run. However if the larger project sees three times as many people, its cost per user will be lower and it will be more efficient.

However it is not always a matter of the biggest or the cheapest being the best, especially when the service is intended to reach a particular group of people. Both centres might be aimed at giving advice to tenants on an estate on the edge of the town. The large project in the town centre might see 100 people per week, of whom 10 come from the target area. The local project might only see 30 people per week, but all of them coming from the local area. In this case the second one is more efficient in reaching more people in the target group for a week's effort, and the cost per target user will now be lower.

Effectiveness is about making the desired changes. Here the relationship is between the inputs and the outcomes – what happened. Staying with the example of the housing advice centre, the centre is effective if the people getting advice find it helpful and they can use it to get repairs done or prevent a problem getting worse. We can still talk about 'how many' and use numbers when describing effectiveness and quality – for example, "75% of users benefited in the following ways ..."

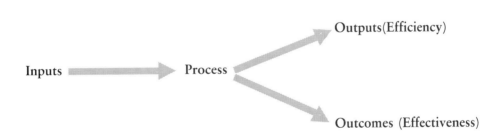

SETTING QUALITY INDICATORS

Many staff and managers in voluntary organisations, as in other agencies, stress the importance of the quality of their services, but often it is not clear what is meant by quality. Before launching into monitoring and evaluation of activities or planning new services it is a good idea to consider what is a good quality service in the circumstances of this particular project. Various approaches have been developed by researchers and consultants. Some are suggested here and these can be used separately or in combination. The first two involve people within the project, such as staff, volunteers and managers, while the third one is wider and brings in other people's perspectives, especially the users'. There are other ways of addressing the quality of social care projects and some of the books suggested in the list at Part 3 cover this.

1. Good Case/Bad Case

Each person thinks of a real case where they think the project gave a good service or there was a good outcome. List out what was especially good about it. Then compare the various lists, and draw out what everyone agrees is a good quality service. It is also important to discuss any aspects where the lists appear to contradict each other, or suggest things that are not generally agreed.

Each person also looks at a case which did not work, or where you thought the project did not give a particularly good service, and again list out why. Compare these in the same way as for the 'good case' list. Here the features of good quality are what would have put matters right or the opposite of what actually happened. This is sometimes much more revealing than the 'good case' lists.

From the two sets of lists and the related discussion you are trying to get an agreed list of features of a good quality service for your situation which all the people involved – staff, volunteers and managers – can share and work towards.

2. Ideal Outcomes

Again think of some real cases, perhaps some new referrals, or fictitious typical cases. Note down what you hope the project would be able to do in an ideal world and what the best possible outcome would be. Again compare lists with colleagues. It is also useful to discuss this with other people who work in similar circumstances. From this you are trying to identify factors which can be applied to your project and which set high standards for the kind of services you provide or the kind of people with whom you work. Think about how your project could be developed and adapted to provide the best possible service.

3. Three Good Things

Every person who can be roped into the exercise – staff, managers, volunteers, users, the professionals with whom you work – notes three things which they think indicate a good quality service for this type of project. This can be done on postcard-sized index cards or bits of paper, or on the coloured stick-notes, which can then be posted into a box or stuck on the wall.

Again, the idea is to draw out of these suggestions factors which everyone agrees is associated with a good quality service and then to find ways of discussing the things that there is some disagreement about so that an agreed list can be used.

Points to Note

• It is always a good idea to check out with other people what we mean by 'good quality' or what we mean by a 'successful' service or outcome, and not just involve those who share our own point of view. Sometimes it makes sense for the management committee or co-ordinator or just a few key people to start this off, but you need to then involve other people, check out your ideas and expand and refine them.

• Check that your performance indicators or quality assurance measures cover all aspects of the project and do not just focus on one or two features. One way is to think through the whole pattern of what you are doing.

Inputs:	Numbers and types of people involved such as staff and volunteers: are people leaving, not coming, staying too long?
	Types of people – balance of age and gender, people from ethnic minorities, etc: how do they reflect the views of our users?
	The circumstances of our users: are we reaching those with the greatest need?
	Practical resources, such as buildings, transport, meals etc: are they good enough? Accessible?
Process:	What we do: the range of activities
	Numbers of visits or contacts per client
	Relationships between staff and volunteers and users
	The way in which the project is managed and organised: support group meetings for volunteers and staff, internal information arrangements.
Outputs:	The level of service given to users.
	Number of leaflets or reports produced etc.

Outcomes: What has changed: what have people learned? The changes in their circumstances.

What was most useful for them? Did they want other things which were not provided?

What were the benefits for other agencies?

PART TWO:
PUTTING IT INTO PRACTICE

1

Getting Started: Planning for Monitoring and Evaluation

Perhaps the most important stage of any monitoring and evaluation work is the initial stage of planning what will be done. Often the need to monitor and evaluate is highlighted by the funder's requirements and there is a risk that the arrangements do not take full account of the information needs of the project itself. Similarly, a project may want to gather information to answer a specific query or deal with a particular case or circumstance, but not stop to assess this in the context of other information needs.

The research study found that monitoring and evaluation tend to be thought of as something separate from other activities, both on a day-to-day basis and in longer-term development and planning. However, as the report shows, monitoring and evaluation of service delivery and outcomes are important elements of good management. They need to be considered along with other activities and become part of managing the quality of services and ensuring the best possible use is made of the available resources. Where it is tacked on this is likely to result in duplication of effort (the same information recorded several times for several purposes), in limited use being made of information and gaps in the points covered. Even when an organisation has good monitoring and evaluation arrangements it is useful to review these periodically, and then to check that the current arrangements still meet the needs of both the project itself and the people outside (managers, funders and referrers) and that information is being gathered in the most cost-effective way. It is also important to ensure that monitoring arrangements have not become an end in themselves and that the

15

functioning of the overall project and/or of particular parts is still being critically reviewed.

Another reason for carrying out an initial planning exercise is to start off the monitoring and evaluation work with a high level of commitment from the people who will be carrying this out. The findings of the research study have clearly shown that when project staff believe in the value of the monitoring and evaluation work they are much more likely to complete it on time. Other factors which help the work along include the level of commitment and support from managers and knowing what information funders and referrers will be looking for in any assessment they make of the functioning and value of the project. Some thought needs to be given to whether to involve these people in planning the monitoring and evaluation work and how to take account of the views and interests of the various groups. This is discussed in detail below.

The third reason for carrying out a review of this sort is its value in highlighting any underlying problems affecting the project. One example is the relevance of formal aims and objectives. Most projects keep to their original aims but, over time, the relevance or relative priority of these aims and objectives can change. Indeed, it could be argued that a healthy project is one which continues to reflect the needs and interests of its users, rather than one which rigidly sticks to its original remit, irrespective of changing circumstances. It is useful to review the relevance of aims and objectives before embarking upon an evaluation which will use these as the criteria of the effectiveness of the project. A careful consideration of the purpose and remit of a project is something which should take place from time to time in any case, and is part of the on-going responsibility and function of managers.

The notes at the end of this section give a checklist for planning for monitoring and evaluation. These take account of ideas developed with projects participating in this fieldwork. There is also a list of practical points which have been found to ease this process. Perhaps the most important of these was the use of an "Issue Sheet". As most projects worked through this checklist they identified points which gave them problems or which they considered particularly important, which any monitoring and evaluation exercise would need to address. One example might be where there was a conflict between the stated formal aims and objectives and the way in which the project was now working.

SCOPE OF INITIAL PLANNING STAGE

The research study showed that projects are more likely to successfully carry out monitoring and evaluation of their services if this is done in a way that suits their circumstances and needs. The planning stage is the essential first step in this process. This flexibility around each project's circumstances has implications, especially for those people managing and funding the projects.

Since this approach is based on the needs and circumstances of individual projects, the monitoring and evaluation package that they identify will be specific to them. Projects might be willing to use standard approaches to particular problems. However, it cannot be assumed that if, for example, two day care centres for people with learning difficulties undertake this planning for monitoring and evaluation they will identify the same set of needs, give them the same priority and gather the information in the same way. If a funder wishes the project to use the same approach as others in the area, they would have to point the project to this or make this a specific requirement. In the same way, it should not be assumed that two projects which are part of the same organisation will gather all points of information in exactly the same way unless this has been specifically drawn to their attention or they have agreed this approach and definitions etc together. For many purposes it will not matter that two organisations get to a broadly similar point by different routes, provided each is comfortable with their approach and it meets all the demands that are put on it.

It needs to be understood that this planning exercise is an integral preliminary stage and cannot substitute for actually checking information, analysing and interpreting results: it is not a replacement for the monitoring and evaluation itself. However, the exercise itself can be expected to show if the project is generally fulfilling, or failing to meet, its aims and objectives. Inevitably, if the project is faced with the conclusion that generally things are not going as well as they might have expected, this is likely to pose some problems for them in the short to medium term. Following this through and assessing exactly how and why things are out of kilter through rigorous monitoring and evaluation will be invaluable in helping that project fully understand where the problems are created and then plan for the future and put matters to right. The problem is that if the project staff become de-motivated or feel threatened, they are unlikely to be able to take these steps. Managers, and perhaps funders and referrers, need to be aware of the possibility of this and to be ready to take appropriate measures.

A review of project work along these lines can also be expected to highlight issues beyond monitoring and evaluation. Examples which arose in the study were problems in the volume of work of level of staffing, tensions between the project and practice or policies of some sections in the Social Work Department or Health Board, and matters to do with wider policy or legislative provision for this group of users. Inevitably, many projects will want to do something about these issues, such as entering into negotiations with the local authority or other voluntary organisations in the area or spending more time on campaigning. One practical consequence, however, is that the project may feel torn between carrying out the monitoring and evaluation work – in order to prove their case or establish the scale of a problem – and wanting to do something about the problem that they have already identified. It may be more appropriate for someone else, such as the Chair of the Management Committee, to start initial discussions with the referrers or other agencies while the project staff focus on the provision of services to users and monitoring and evaluation.

WHO SHOULD BE INVOLVED IN PLANNING MONITORING AND EVALUATION?

The people who need to be involved in planning monitoring and evaluation are:

- those who have particular questions which the monitoring and evaluation will need to answer; and
- those who will be carrying out the day-to-day monitoring tasks.

It therefore follows that the mix of people involved in planning monitoring and evaluation for any one project will depend on the circumstances of that project, and that different people might be involved in rather different ways.

For most projects in the research study the planning for monitoring and evaluation was a collaborative process that took place over a month or so. Typically, a project would take the views of managers, users, funders and referrers and staff, pull these together in a planning day which involved mostly members of the project, and then check out the fine details with the various interested groups before launching on the work. A possible model for this is illustrated below.

A few projects decided to involve people other than those in the basic staff group, which sometimes included volunteers. The main types of people involved were managers, users, funders and other professionals with whom they worked, such as their main referrers. From the experience of projects participating in this fieldwork and commenting on the methods which emerged, a list of advantages and disadvantages of involving each of these groups of people has been developed.

Entire Staff Team

Advantages

Staff are more likely to have a commitment to monitoring and evaluation work if they are a part of the process of planning the work and setting the agenda. In particular, each person will understand why the work is being done and how it will be used.

May get better quality of work, such as consistency in how information is recorded, although involvement in the planning stage is not sufficient to guarantee this.

The Action Plan (range of work to be done, priorities and timescales) is more likely to be realistic as staff can point out any likely problems.

Disadvantages

The staff group may be too large for meaningful discussion.

Involving everyone may mean closing the project or not giving a service to some users.

If the project has staff (paid and volunteer) from a wide range of roles and backgrounds, some people may feel marginalised or excluded from the discussion (language used, people interested only in their part of the project) or the project may focus on some aspects and disregard others (eg direct care aspects but not resource and staff management issues).

Manager
Advantages

The manager is able to link day-to-day work to overall aims and advantages – "an informed overview".

She/he can make sure time is available to the project to carry out agreed monitoring and evaluation work.

She/he can authorise changes to take place immediately within project (so staff will feel that something is happening, see overall monitoring and evaluation as positive).

A manager can make sure the later outcomes of the evaluation are taken on, such as negotiating with funders, changes to balance of activities by project.

Managers may bring greater awareness and experience of people outside organisation – for example, who to link into in local authority for policy matters, likely funding options and so implications for services, specialist advice or training inputs.

They can take up any issues arising from the planning stage with other managers (Senior Managers, other Committee Members, colleagues) such as emerging problems that could be more widespread, alert them to decisions that will need to be taken.

They can make links with other parts of organisation's work or similar projects elsewhere.

Disadvantages

If a manager is included in the main planning discussion, staff may be less honest and open about problems which monitoring and evaluation has to address.

Any on-going management/staff disagreements might spill over – for example, conflict over a small issue such as mileage rates deflecting attention away from important matters.

The manager may not be sufficiently objective about the project, especially if they were closely involved in planning and setting it up and managing or running it in the early stages ("too close to their baby").

Comparisons with other projects may be unhelpful: for example take attention away from needs of this project; the monitoring and evaluation could end up taking on the needs of other projects, or it could be assumed that the timescales, resources and skills etc needed for the monitoring and evaluation will be the same as for other projects.

It may be too easy for the project to short-circuit the evaluation since the manager can implement change if convinced of need – in effect, to jump straight to the solution to an apparent problem before it has been confirmed and the scale of the problem, users' views etc have been established.

Users (Including Former Users, Carers)
Advantages

Builds in the user perspective from the outset – users helping to set the agenda rather than only responding to questions raised by service providers.

Users can challenge professionals' assumptions – for example, on the criteria for measuring the effectiveness of the project.

It is more likely to lead to users carrying out part of the monitoring and evaluation work and to participating in elements which involve them – such as a survey of users' views, doing a large-scale survey of local people.

If users are involved from the outset the research is likely to be better – for example, in the language and content of questionnaires. (This is discussed in greater detail in the report on the Putting People First project – see reading list).

Gives users more understanding of how the project functions beyond day-to-day matters and involves them in longer-term planning. This can be especially important when the project aims to involve users in running services or ultimately to hand over the project to local management.

If the project holds a general meeting of all users to discuss issues concerning the monitoring and evaluation this can also be used to discuss other matters. If this is followed by action on part of the project, people are likely to think of the exercise as positive.

Disadvantages

Again, staff may feel restricted about raising some issues, especially if these might cause worry or distress, such as the risk of the grant not being renewed and of the service closing or raising expectations that may not be met. If users are involved in the planning day this may have limited value and be followed by a second meeting when other issues ("the real agenda") are discussed.

Most projects will include only a few people as representatives of other users in any meeting or planning day. The users may be inhibited by the number of staff and other professionals involved, the language used etc, and there could be a risk of tokenism.

Users may be resistant to any prospect of change. As a result, the emphasis may be on demonstrating the value of the project rather than on ways of making the service better.

Any user involvement in planning the evaluation could duplicate or compromise arrangements already established under that local authority's consultation processes.

Referrers, Funders, Other Professionals
Advantages

Outsiders may bring a different perspective on the project and related issues, such as a wider and/or more detached view, putting the project in the context of policy and practice development.

They can explain and clarify the interests and information needs of themselves and colleagues, explain the way projects are assessed and the criteria used.

They could comment on the possible scope for changes to the existing information system (eg how statistics are collected and feedback) or to the services provided (eg is it worth doing a feasibility study for extending into a new area or would this not be supported anyway).

Involvement in planning the monitoring and evaluation could help develop and build on close working relationships, put a partnership into practical effect and promote feelings of mutual trust. The people concerned may be more committed to doing part of the monitoring and can explain this to colleagues – such as a survey of their views, providing information on outcomes for shared clients or on people not receiving a service from the project.

The funding and referring organisations may be more likely to accept and support any report and conclusions reached from the later evaluation if a key person was part of setting the agenda and planning details of the information collection and assessment process.

Disadvantages

Again, staff may feel inhibited about admitting to problems or criticising that person's colleagues or organisation.

As with some managers, someone who was closely involved in planning and developing the project may be too close to it, or to the original idea, to be objective or to consider any options which might lead to change.

The person may not know about such matters as policies, funding mechanisms or how statistics are used. This will depend on the person's status within the authority, personal knowledge and experience and how the relevant funders and/or referrers organise themselves. This may not matter if the project understands the limitations on the person's input, but there is a risk of the project assuming the person carries expertise and relying on this in a way that is perhaps not intended. (This is discussed more fully in Chapter 5 of the research report.)

There is a risk of the monitoring and evaluation being overtaken or weighted by issues of concern to the referrer or funder rather than to the project.

Who Should be Involved: Summing Up

Any projects embarking on an exercise of this sort need to take account of their own circumstances and the relative advantages and disadvantages of involving each of these types of people when considering who to involve at this initial planning stage. In some circumstances it will be a good idea to have people with whom the project works closely, such as the line manager or a referrer, carrying out this planning exercise along with the project staff. Elsewhere, projects might consider it more appropriate to consult these people in separate discussions, as was done by the great majority of projects participating in the research study. It also may be appropriate to limit this exercise to the project staff the first time it is done but involve other people in subsequent reviews of the monitoring or evaluation arrangements, when the initial problems and tensions have been ironed out and/or the project staff feel more confident about discussing these openly.

There are many steps which projects can take to achieve as many of the advantages and as few of the disadvantages listed above as possible.

For the *staff group*, if this is more than about 12-15 people having everyone at a single planning meeting is not feasible. However, a project could divide the discussion to cover self-contained parts of the work, with each group of staff

Inputs to Planning, Monitoring and Evaluation

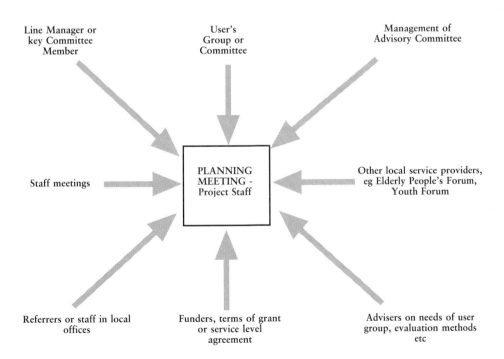

23

C

reviewing their activities and information needs and a representative from each feeding this into the plan for the overall project. Staff can also discuss this through other channels – for example, at regular meetings – and then feed in written comments, with the combined lists later checked back.

Rather than close the project completely, in some situations staff could explain to users in advance that they can only deal with emergencies on that day. Another option is to get someone in to "hold the fort" – for example, a worker from another project, a manager, or someone from the local authority as part of the supportive partnership relationship.

On many occasions it will be difficult to involve *users* in a specific planning meeting, because people have other commitments during office hours, or because attending meetings is limited by the availability of public transport or by the need to care for children or other people. Again, it may be possible to link a consultation process into other meetings or events. Other options would include providing resources such as transport and child care. A range of ways of enabling service users to be involved in assessing the quality of services has been developed by the Birmingham Special Action Project.

It should also be remembered that monitoring and evaluation are parts of an on-going cycle. Views expressed by *users* and by *referrers and other professionals* will inform the next stage of the evaluation and planning process, including the planning of other surveys. It may be a good idea to have an initial survey of users, for example, as part of a preliminary stage of identifying ideas, which then feeds in to planning the main monitoring and evaluation exercise.

One of the findings of this research study is that staff in Social Work Departments and other bodies with different roles and responsibilities – care to individual clients, strategic planning, administration of the financial side of grants to voluntary projects – looked for different things from projects' evaluations. It will often be advisable to check with all relevant parts of an organisation that their interests are known – for example, involving a social worker from the local office with whom the project works closely in the planning meeting and then writing to the Area Manager and Grants Section with the list of things you plan to cover.

Role of Facilitator

For the fieldwork projects the researcher was usually involved in these planning meetings, mostly taking the role of a facilitator as well as adviser on monitoring and evaluation methods. Early feedback from project staff was that it was helpful to have someone in this facilitator role, which was then refined and different ways of doing this were developed.

The main features of the role identified as helpful to the planning process in itself, and as the foundation for the subsequent monitoring and evaluation work, were having someone:

- to keep the day or process running to time, and especially ensuring that an Action Plan was agreed;
- who did not have to think about detailed points and could take an overview;
- who was not part of the project and so had no vested interests;
- was able to respond objectively to points raised and follow-up and clarify when necessary – for example, any inconsistencies;
- to check out points being noted and the agreed Action Plan with all the people involved to make sure they were in agreement or that disagreements were discussed appropriately;
- who understands if the meeting has a dual purpose – for example also for team building, or to discuss and resolve a particular internal issue – and keeps this and the monitoring and evaluation aspects in their proper context;
- who is aware of the significance of wider dimensions – such as funding mechanisms and wider policy matters (although not necessarily of the details) and can check these have been considered.

In some cases in the research study this role was undertaken by a manager. This was successful in a few instances, but generally it was felt to be inconsistent with the "bottom-up" project-centred approach of the evaluation of services by projects. Other people who were identified as potentially taking on this role included:

- another manager within the organisation;
- a Development Officer from an intermediary body;
- an academic or consultant;
- some specific colleagues from another voluntary organisation or project who were experienced in service-related matters and had done their own monitoring and evaluation.

As with the decision about who to involve in the planning process, the decision on whether a facilitator is needed at all, and if so who that should be, will depend on the circumstances of the project and the range of options available in that area.

CARRYING OUT A PLANNING REVIEW

The rest of this section outlines the way these initial reviews to plan for the monitoring and evaluation work were carried out.

There is a checklist of the main points and questions to be covered, along with a list of practical steps to make this easier and a possible timetable. Like the other parts of this guide, these are suggestions based on the experience of the projects which helped with the fieldwork for this study. They are only starting points and can be adapted to reflect your circumstances.

There are then two Case Examples, describing typical situations for projects and illustrating how the planning stage was handled in each case. One shows a straightforward situation, involving a new project, where the planning was done by the project team. The second is a more complicated scenario when more people are involved and the planning is done over a longer period.

PLANNING FOR MONITORING AND EVALUATION: CHECKLIST

1 Consider aims and objectives

List both formal statement and team's perceptions of what the project is there to achieve.

Do you want to add anything which is not in the formal aims, such as raising the awareness of the local authority or a campaigning role?

What are the relative priorities if there are several elements to project?

If anything is not clear, or if there are disagreements or concerns, note these on an Issue sheet.

2 List out in detail:

Who the project works with

[for example users, carers or parents, local community, a list of other agencies].

What it does

[for example, list of activities, advice, advocating for users, liaison with other agencies, other services linked to or organised through the project].

Why it does this, changes which you want to make: the intended outputs and outcomes.

Check:

- is there any group of people for whom project is not doing anything?

- are there any activities for which there are no clear users or no reasons?
- are there any intended outcomes for which nothing is being done to move things on?
- If so, note these on the Issues sheet.

3. List out all the things you need to know about the project

Use lists at 2. as a check and take account of points on the Issues sheet.

Think through for:

- the project's own needs;
- information needs of the wider voluntary organisation, eg Management Committee, any central Policy Section, fundraisers;
- other agencies' information requirements – funders, referrers, organisations to which the project is affiliated.

If you are not clear what another person or agency will want you to tell them about your project, make arrangements to check this.

4 Check what is gathered already

Mark what is already gathered, including where and how this is done. This can be very wide, for example, case records, transport list, staff and volunteer rotas, staff diaries, telephone and/or mail booking system etc.

Is anything being collected that there does not seem to be a use for or is being duplicated?

5 Plan how to fill in the gaps and make best use of what is already there

Can existing information systems be simplified or made easier to handle? – eg revising the referral forms to a "tick box" layout for easier collation for routine statistics.

Can existing systems be adapted to cover any of the gaps? – for example, adding an extra item to referral forms.

If new things are needed, consider what you need and how this can be met – for example, self-evaluation models listed in this handbook, advice from someone.

Is there anyone whom you could consult, such as staff in another voluntary organisation which has already set up monitoring and evaluation arrangements?

6 Agree an Action Plan

Priorities: greatest urgency? importance? easiest thing first?

Who is taking on responsibility for what.

Timetable: allowing plenty of preparation time and space for things to take longer than expected.

Review of monitoring and evaluation arrangements.

PLANNING FOR MONITORING AND EVALUATION: PRACTICAL STEPS

Timescale

It is helpful to set aside most of a working day for this exercise. The experience of projects participating in this study was that having to pick up an unfinished planning/review exercise at a later date was difficult and unproductive, but sometimes this will be the best option. When a project's information needs are straightforward and there are unlikely to be strong differences in staff's views – which will usually be the case in circumstances like Case Example 1 or for any subsequent reviews of monitoring arrangements after the initial round – half a day should be long enough.

From the experience of this study, a timetable with space for some time saving or wider discussion on issues highlighted would be that given here. However, this should be flexible and accommodate the needs of that project.

10.00 – 10.20   Introduction; Why project needs to monitor and evaluate its work; What is meant by monitoring and evaluation.

10.20 – 11.00	Aims and Objectives [1].
11.00 – 12.00	Who the project works with, activities, intended outcomes [2]*.
12.00 – 12.30	Check for gaps, identify and discuss any issues from this [2].
12.30 – 13.30	Break for lunch, phone messages, etc.
13.30 – 13.45	Recap/fresh look at Aims and current work.
13.45 – 14.15	List of things project needs to know [3]*.
14.15 – 14.45	Check against what is already available [4].
14.45 – 15.15	Plan to fill gaps [5].
15.15 – 15.45	Agree action plan [6].

* For a large project, these stages could be separated for each part or group of staff and then pulled together.

Location

The location can be anywhere convenient where the project can divert or minimise interruptions. Most fieldwork projects did this within their own premises but a few borrowed a room from the local Council of Social Services or used another location away from interruptions.

Equipment, etc

Have a flip chart, drawing pins or another means of making several sheets visible [for checking one list against others] and several colours of pens/markers. If possible, make arrangements for tea, coffee etc which will minimise interruptions to discussion.

Working through the Plan

It often helps if different members of the group take turns to write points identified or agreed by the group on the flip chart sheets.

When going over the lists to check if there are any gaps or overlaps, use a different coloured pen to mark these.

Similarly, use different colours to mark off items in the list of points the project needs to know that are already available and write in the actual source(s) of this information.

When setting priorities for the Action Plan, it is often better to start with what is easiest to collect and analyse, rather than the most important. This is usually quicker in the long run as you learn over an easier task and staff will be encouraged by having results fairly early on.

It is useful to get the sheets typed up and/or keep them stored so they can be referred to later on as the monitoring and evaluation progresses.

Reviewing Arrangements: The next round

As noted before, monitoring and evaluation are part of a continuous cycle and are an integral, on-going part of good management. They are not separate, self-contained tasks. Most projects will in any case want to refine their monitoring arrangements after the first round of monitoring and evaluation and then as the project develops or circumstances change. It is a good idea to plan to review these arrangements every 6 or 12 months or so. Even if the project's manager(s) were not involved in day-to-day monitoring and evaluation it is helpful if they are involved at the review stage as part of their management responsibilities.

CASE EXAMPLE 1

Planning monitoring and evaluation in straightforward circumstances

Background

This was a new project, where staff had been in post for 3-4 months, referrals were beginning to come in and direct service delivery was about to begin. The project was directly based on a well-established scheme in another town and the detailed specification, which included a very clear set of aims and objectives, had been discussed at length with the main funding and referring agencies.

At this stage there were four staff members: the co-ordinator, two project workers and a part-time secretary. Both the co-ordinator and secretary had used information systems in similar situations before.

What was done

This project planned their monitoring and evaluation arrangements without consulting other people as they felt the expectations for this were already clearly stated. The manager discussed the general need for such a system in the course of routine meetings with the staff and asked to be kept informed of plans and progress.

The detailed arrangements were discussed and agreed at a meeting of the staff specifically organised to plan the monitoring and evaluation. The aim was to complete this in a morning to reflect the secretary's working hours. In the event this was done in under three hours and staff felt they had enough time to discuss matters fully. They commented that the reasons they found this straightforward were that they had already discussed the major issues at some length during their initial training and settling in phase and shared a high level of commitment to meeting the needs of their user group.

Afterwards the co-ordinator checked the plans with the manager at their regular meeting. The monitoring arrangements were started immediately.

An Advisory Group, which covered representatives of the other agencies with whom the project worked, was established and met for the first time about a month later. The Group was informed of the arrangements, which only involved project staff at this stage. The referrers/funders were content with the way this process was done, seeing responsibility for monitoring activities and quality of service as part of the management of the project. However, the plan is to involve the Advisory Group to a greater extent as the project develops.

This chart shows the way these inputs came together.

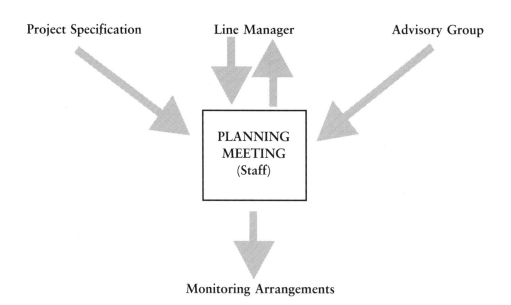

CASE EXAMPLE 2

Planning monitoring and evaluation in complicated circumstances

Background

This was a Neighbourhood Resource Centre, offering support and services to families in the local area. The project was originally funded under the Urban Aid Programme, which placed major emphasis on improving the physical environment and developing effective inter-agency working. Over the next six years the demands on the project had changed in response to other initiatives and policies affecting the area, new families with different needs, etc. On two occasions it had been agreed between the project and the funding agencies to change the priority given to elements of the objectives and activities. People often spoke of the 'old project' and the 'new project' as if they were completely separate.

The project was now coming to the end of this funding arrangement. The local authority had discussed the role they would like to see for the project with the organisation. Before any new arrangement could be decided, however, there would need to be a review, which would draw on any description and evaluation of services submitted by the project.

The project had a large staff group of 16, including several people who worked part-time or were sessional workers or volunteers. A few staff had been with the project since the beginning and had strong feelings about activities which the project had given up.

Over the years the project had established or joined a complex network of consultation, advisory and planning groups. There was a strong commitment to user involvement, although many people stayed in the area for only a short while and/or had personal difficulties that took up a large part of their energies. There were neighboorhood/user meetings at the project and issues raised through any channel were taken up. Two users were members of the project's Advisory Group and they tried to sound out the view of other users.

What was done

The co-ordinator discussed the range of topics the project wanted to raise and the achievements they wanted to show with all the staff and volunteers in the course of regular meetings. At these it was decided that the volunteers and sessional workers would prefer not be involved in further planning, but were happy to be involved in activities like surveys of users. The co-ordinator also discussed the scope of the monitoring and evaluation with the Advisory Group and another key person in the Local Authority.

The core staff group and the manager held a special day's meeting to discuss the monitoring and evaluation. This involved 8 people, excluding the researcher. During the course of working through a review of the project's current activities, identifying information needs and planning how these would be met, the staff were able to express their views on the changes to the project that had occurred and were planned. This had been identified by the co-ordinator as an issue from the earlier discussions and the target agenda and timetable for the day had taken this into account.

After this group of project staff had agreed the main points, this list was referred back to the other staff and Advisory Group at the next round of regular meetings, partly to get their views but also because it was hoped to survey local professionals about their experience of the project. The co-ordinator and manager also checked that this would meet the requirements of the main future funder.

The final package of information gathering – users' views, outcomes of recent cases, etc – was that identified by the staff at the planning day, while the funders had suggested a few extra points to be covered in the evaluation. All the staff were kept informed about what had been agreed and notices were put up at the project telling users that the project would be conducting surveys etc to help improve services and to include users' views in the report to the Local Authority.

One consequence of this level of consultation was that nearly four months was spent on planning the monitoring before any work began. At the time this caused some worry as the funder's decision-making timetable could not be altered and there was a deadline for completion of all the work and submission of a report. In the event, the project met the deadlines. The information gathering and evaluation of their work by the project went smoothly and ran closely to the planned timescales and feedback from staff in the funding and referring agencies on the report was constructive. Afterwards, the co-ordinator and staff thought that the reasons for this included the care taken in planning the review, the involvement of the staff throughout the process and level of consultation with colleagues from other agencies.

The chart shows the consultation and planning process for this project.

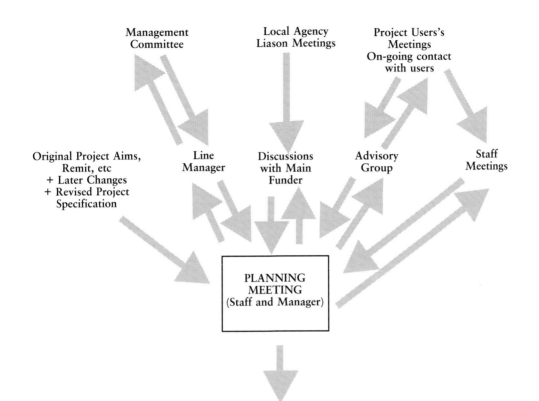

Management
Committee

Local Agency
Liason Meetings

Project Users's
Meetings
On-going contact
with users

Original Project Aims,
Remit, etc
+ Later Changes
+ Revised Project
Specification

Line
Manager

Discussions
with Main
Funder

Advisory
Group

Staff
Meetings

PLANNING
MEETING
(Staff and Manager)

Monitoring and Evaluation Arrangements

2

Who Uses our Services?: Scale and Pattern of Use

WHY WE NEED TO KNOW THIS

All service providers need to have some idea of how many people use their services. This helps us to plan how we are going to provide the service – for example how many volunteers do we need to recruit, how many workers need to be available at certain times? It is also an indicator of the quality of the service – if people stop coming it suggests that something is wrong, while on the other hand if the numbers of users increase it suggests at least something is appreciated.

This is linked to knowing who uses a service – the balance between men and women; the ages of the users; how many are local or from outwith the area.

It is also a good idea to know something of the pattern of use. Do the same people keep coming back? Are the regular users different from the casual or infrequent users?

This is probably the most basic element of monitoring. It is also the starting point for most other types of information such as gathering users' views or identifying the outcomes of the services for users. In the research study 19 of the 26 projects looked at some aspect of monitoring the scale and pattern of use made of the services. All of the projects which did not look at this already had a good system.

The way in which a project monitors the scale and pattern of use made of services will of course depend on its circumstances. Sometimes we need to know *exactly* how many people have used the service or have certain characteristics. Other times a broad estimate will do. As a general rule, the more precise and complete the information that is available about users, the more helpful this will be. Projects might like to check what level of detail is needed for their own purposes and for other people's, such as their funders and referrers.

Some projects will find it much easier to identify the scale and pattern of use of their services than will others. The chart lists factors which the research study found made a difference and gives easy and difficult circumstances for each factor.

Ease of identifying scale and pattern of use

Factor	Easy	Difficult
Initial contact	Standard referral and/or assessment process	Range of referral/contact routes.
		Users self-select: self referrals and informal referrals.
		No or minimal preliminary assessment.
Scale of use	Fixed number or narrow range of people/places at any given time.	No limit on number of people/places.
Accessibility	Service only available on specified days/times.	Lengthy periods when open to users.
	Physical access for target users limited or can be monitored (eg receptionist)	Physical access easy, not monitored (eg several entrances).
Pattern of Service	Fixed package or agreed/negotiated at outset with user	Open-ended for frequency and/or length of contact.
	Users come to project, or project to them, at pre-set times	Contact with project is flexible and user-initiated.
	Contact is service-initiated	
Focus on Service	On a specified person as main user	Potentially on several people within families, all with different needs.
Range of services	Single form of service	Range of services or activities. Not all activities provided by main project.

Typical projects at the "easy" end of the range are:

- day care centres for mentally confused older people, where there is a set number of places, a formal referral and assessment system, transport is provided to bring clients to and home from the centre and if any client did not attend this was noted and followed up immediately;
- long-term residential care for people with disabilities;
- volunteers teaching children a sport or to play a musical instrument on a one to one basis.

At the other extreme, typical projects which find it difficult to note the scale and pattern of use include:

- services working with both users and their carers – for example, children and parents, frail older people and their families or neighbours;
- telephone advice or counselling services;
- drop-in neighbourhood projects such as community centres, and informal day care provision;
- family conciliation services where parents can return to the service for advice or conciliation if subsequent problems arise after the initial contact.

Few projects have features which are all in the "easy" or "difficult" columns noted in the chart. It may be helpful to think of this as a range and to consider each element separately. Figure A shows an example of how a respite care and support service of families with children with disabilities might look, while Figure B shows a day care centre for older people based in a community centre. Both are typical of the kinds of situations many voluntary organisations deal with.

Figure A: Respite care and support for families of children with disabilities

Factor: Feature of Project	Ease of Noting Scale and Pattern of Use		
	Easy	*Medium*	*Difficult*
INITIAL CONTACT: referrals mostly from social work or health care sources: all assessed by project	X		
SCALE OF USE: number of overnight places limited: number of families on books or receiving other care more open, but effective upper limit set.	X ——————— X		
ACCESSIBILITY: all overnight places or visits booked; telephone calls etc from parents channelled through main worker	X		
PATTERN OF SERVICE: flexible, reflecting families' and children's needs		X	
FOCUS OF SERVICE: aim is to give support to all members of family			X
RANGE OF SERVICES: overnight and day care; advice and counselling; support groups for parents and siblings		X ——————— X	

D

Figure B: Drop-in centre for older people attached to a community centre

Factor: Feature of Project	Ease of Noting Scale and Pattern of Use		
	Easy	Medium	Difficult
INITIAL CONTACT: referrals from any source: users self-select; project identifies people needing extra support from within users, including many directly referred by statutory agencies (*)	(X)*		X
SCALE: large use of main day care centre; limited number getting targeted support (*) other care more open, but effective upper limit set.	(X)*		X
ACCESSIBILITY: open 5 days per week and several evenings; easy access to new open-plan building: some of frailer members use transport provided by project (*)		(X)*	X
PATTERN OF SERVICE: user initiated; special inputs initiated mostly by project (*)		(X)*	X
FOCUS OF SERVICE: only on users	X		
RANGE OF SERVICES: wide – personal care, leisure, social, skills classes etc; welfare rights advice etc service run by other agency; some leisure activities arranged through main community centre			X

The way in which a project needs to tackle monitoring the scale and pattern of use largely depends on where it comes on the spectrum.

For projects mostly at the "easy" end, it is likely that existing record keeping systems will be sufficient. The issue here may be ease of recording and especially data extraction. It is also often a good idea to analyse the information in existing records in greater detail before, or hopefully instead of, launching into a changed information system or fresh data collection.

With projects mostly at the difficult end, it may be possible to focus on particular subgroups. Example B is typical of many day care centres for older people and other open, community-based services where the bulk of staff's time and effort is probably spent with a core of more vulnerable users. Here it would be sensible – and probably more appropriate – to start with looking at the scale and pattern of use of this special sub-group and have a less intensive monitoring and evaluation system for the user group as a whole. In Example B, the ease of establishing the pattern of use by all users are of the most dependent users are noted separately. Projects in this type of situation might find it useful to think of the service in this way when planning monitoring and evaluation, rather than only thinking of the service as a whole.

HOW TO DO THIS

Within the research study three main approaches were identified to improving the monitoring of the scale and pattern of use made of projects' services.

1. Streamlining existing records to make best use of information already available.

This was the most frequently used approach. In many projects there was a set of information items on each user: an initial letter or note of a telephone call from the person who first referred the user, notes of any meeting or assessment interview with the user, notes on whatever service arrangement was agreed and notes on any changes that were subsequently made to this – for example expanding care by another day per week. Sometimes projects kept this together for each user, while in others these items were scattered – for example where the referral and assessment papers were kept separately from current notes on service delivery.

The main objectives here were:

- to ease the amount of time and effort put in to collating information – for example, for annual reviews of the service or reports to funders – and

- to make for easier comparisons between the characteristics of the users and/or reasons why they were referred and the service that was then given.

This in turn formed the basis for links made between objectives for individuals and outcomes of delivery of care, which is discussed in more detail in Section 3. In most instances the only change that had to be made to the *content* of information recorded – rather than the layout – was specific identification of the reasons why the person was referred and, in particular, what it was the referrer, the project and user hoped the use of this service would achieve.

Case Examples 3 and 6 show ways in which streamlining the existing records can be helpful.

2. Carrying out more detailed analysis of existing records to address new types of information.

This was done for two main reasons:

- to review the pattern of use of particular services where it would not be possible to go back to the original people to seek further information, and

- where projects wished to monitor the types and rates of referrals coming from different sources. Were social workers and teachers referring different types of children to a youth project, or referring children from different reasons, or were the same types of children cropping up in different places? In the great majority of cases it was possible to address the project's information needs about the scale and pattern of use made of this service and the characteristics of the people who were coming by one or other of these types of work on existing records.

Case Examples 3 and 4 show situations where this was done.

3. Setting up new monitoring systems, especially where the service was initiated by the users.

This arose in settings where the use was largely on a drop-in basis, and it was extremely difficult to track either the overall scale of use or the types of demands and responses for individual users through the methods already at the project's disposal. In each case the use of the service was monitored closely for a short period – normally one or two weeks – which was sufficient to give a fairly detailed and accurate "snapshot" of the pattern of use made at that time. The advantage of this approach was that it gave projects the information which they were seeking and was achievable within their resources. In several instances it was agreed to repeat this at intervals – for example quarterly – to show the changes in patterns of use over time.

This is illustrated in Case Examples 4 and 5.

Remembering to keep a note of what happens every time someone comes in to the project is itself hard work, especially when you are very busy – which is when it is most important. So although this method gives very reliable, useful information about the level of demand on the project it is generally more helpful on an occasional "snapshot" basis than as an every day approach.

CHOOSING A METHOD

The methods of gathering information about the level and pattern of use of your project which are suggested here can be combined with each other and with other arrangements. It all depends on what you need to know and what information you already have.

CASE EXAMPLE 3

Characteristics of users – standard referral/record sheet

Background

Most direct service providers gather information about the circumstances of their users from two sources:

- basic information from other people, often in a written form such as referrals forms or letters; and

- fuller information from the person concerned and any other appropriate people such as the parents of young children, usually gathered through an interview which is often more akin to an informal conversation in style.

Taken together, this information meets three distinct purposes.

1. It allows the project workers or other people to decide whether it is appropriate to offer that person a service.

2. It provides the base for future work if the user is accepted into the project.

3. It gives the information needed for monitoring purposes – for example, the number and circumstances of people accepted, information about waiting lists and information for the annual report.

It is relatively easy to keep the referral form. However, because different people are providing this they will inevitably describe things in slightly different ways. Even when a project provides a form for referrals some people will prefer to put their request in a letter. Others will make referrals verbally – over the phone or at meetings.

Recording the information from the interview often poses even more of a problem. The format usually reflects the type of conversation in being very flexible and open-ended. As a result, different people tend to record information in their own way. This makes it difficult to compare and collate information across the cases later on. Because staff are more concerned with listening to the person than with writing, notes sometimes are rather brief and incomplete. Staff may not feel it is worth recording information if they are not going to be able to offer a service – for example, if the person is outwith their criteria or will only be put on a waiting list.

Even when all the information is pulled together, it can be difficult to relate to this to the other record forms that are used. It is also often difficult to extract material for statistical purposes, such as the annual report.

This is always more of an issue when there is a larger number of people using the project. When the numbers are fairly small staff are more likely to be able to remember any details they forgot to record at the time, and issues about larger numbers of turned away applicants or advice-only cases do not arise. However, when there are substantial numbers of users there is greater scope for things to go awry and greater need for a reliable written information system.

Circumstances of Project

One typical example is a service for young homeless people which is dealing with several hundred enquiries each year.

The project provides short-term hostel-type accommodation for people aged 16-21, with support, practical training and advice to help them find secure accommodation and have the necessary income and skills to sustain this. Residents can stay for a maximum of twelve weeks, although some move on earlier: a tiny minority are asked to leave while others are able to find somewhere to stay or move back to live with a family member, often with help from the project in resolving earlier problems.

When a young person comes to the project a member of staff will have an initial interview/discussion with them. If it is appropriate for them to stay with the project and if a space is available the person will be offered a place. Often there is no available bed, however, and in these circumstances staff can suggest the young person stays in touch in case a vacancy comes up and, if possible, will try to offer practical support in the meantime (for example provide a hot meal, a place to shower and wash clothes).

The project's funding means that it can only work with young people with a local connection with that District and is expected to work mostly with people from several local areas of multi-deprivation. The project places a high emphasis on working closely with local agencies (the social work department, district council housing department, advice agencies, housing association and other groups such as local churches), although many of these have high levels of staff turnover.

As well as offering a direct service this voluntary organisation includes among its aims and objectives a campaigning role. In this, it draws the needs and circumstances of young homeless people to the attention of local and central government departments, tries to educate and change attitudes of the general community.

When a young person or a worker in another agency telephones the project with a referral a member of staff will note any basic information – such as the main circumstances and the name of the person if given. The main purpose at this stage is to establish whether the project can help that person – does the person meet the criteria and can the project offer a place? If things appear to be suitable the young person would then come to the project – usually within an hour or so of the initial contact. Other young people come to the project without any prior warning. In either set of circumstances, a staff member would interview the young person to identify the circumstances more fully and assess them for a place. At the same time, they would offer support and advice.

In these circumstances there was felt to be little point in having a conventional referral form, so the staff devised and used a single form designed around this main interview (see form A). Around three-quarters of all applicants never get to the interview stage, however, because there are no places available. In these circumstances, the staff jotted down a few notes on a form. Usually the member of staff who carried out the interview with the potential user did not record information at that time but would simply note down the main points on a piece of paper. The main priority had to be on responding to the needs of that particular person and getting them settled into the hostel or phoning around to try to find other places if the hostel was full: this could easily take several hours. It was only after this that the member of staff would complete the form. They often found this time consuming, especially when the project was very busy. It was also recognised that staff did tend to miss points of information, especially when the project had not been able to offer the person a service.

Staff found these forms satisfactory for on-going work with those clients who received a service – for example, if they needed to refer back to any of the original details. These forms were supplemented by other notes as time passed and especially at the end of the person's time with the project. When the young person left details were noted of the accommodation which they went onto and other relevant circumstances such as their employment or other income arrangements.

Although useful on a case basis, the information was found to be very unwieldy to pull together for the annual reports and for material on campaigning issues. At the same time, the project found the information system could not answer some specific points: for example, it needed a lot of tracking down against directories to establish the proportion of people living in the areas of multi-deprivation.

What Was Done

Staff were agreed about the range of information that they needed, but they wanted something which was quicker to complete and to analyse. This project had produced two annual reports and from this had identified a range of factors which were shared by most of the users, such as the types of accommodation used before and on leaving the project and reasons for young people becoming homeless. The project team decided that much of the detail which they were writing down on these forms was not needed for record-keeping purposes, although it was still very important to be aware of this in talking to the young person and understanding their circumstances. It was decided to replace the existing referral/interview forms with a simpler form which was almost entirely made up of closed "tick-box" type questions, and this is shown at B.

Some of the ways in which information was recorded were changed. For example, instead of noting the date of birth they decided to note people's ages: this had the advantages of coming over as much less bureaucratic, no calculations were needed and collating information for statistical purposes became much easier. They also decided to add information about the discharge arrangements, so that all relevant information was together on a single sheet. This was placed at the front of the case file for those people who became residents. Because of this, it was decided to move the note of the intended moving out date to the top of the form, so that it was very clear and kept firmly in the mind of the staff and resident when planning the future.

Once these forms were in regular use staff noticed savings in time when completing the information. The main advantage was noted by the person who had responsibility for pulling together the monthly and six-monthly statistical information and preparing the annual report. Because the information was now much easier to collate, the project began to look at more complex analysis – for example, the way in which reasons for homelessness varied according to the age and gender of users. From this, the project has been able to identify issues which have been taken up with the Social Work Department and Housing Department, and have been found to be useful by all agencies in planning for the needs and circumstances of young homeless people in this area.

Applications in other settings

Many projects find it useful to move from an open, descriptive format to a more structured layout. One approach would be to consider whether each point on the existing information form could be turned into categories: for example age-bands, ethnic groups, whether or not people had particular special needs.

For example, in the case of some community care facilities:

	Yes	No
Limited mobility	☐	☐
Limited sight	☐	☐ etc

In this case the project took the opportunity to review the kind of information recorded as well as the format used. Many projects will be content with the range and detail of information requested about referrals/applications but it is still a good idea to re-consider this from time to time. Could we manage without any items? Is there anything missing which it would be useful to know?

The project in this Case Example had a computer with a database package which they used to analyse the referral information. In these circumstances the pre-categorised information was much easier to enter. It would, however, be simple to sort these sheets manually: this is explained at Section 4 of Part 3 of the handbook.

HOMELESSNESS PROJECT : REFERRAL SHEET (A)

Referral number:

Name:

Date of Birth:

Last Address:

(Type if not clear)

Last permanent address (if different)

(Type if not clear)

Local connection :

Referral Agency / Contact:

Homelesssness career:

Reasons for Homelessness:

Family Circumstances:

_____

Contact with Social Work Department
- current contact?

- previous experience of residential care?

_____

Contact with other agencies:

_____

Employment, Training :

_____

Other personal circumstances, Notes:
(eg health, special needs)

REFERRAL FORM   (B)   Referral Number   Moving out Date

Project Response :   ☐ Accepted   ☐ Outwith criteria   ☐ No place available

Female :   ☐ 16   ☐ 17   ☐ 18   ☐ 19   ☐ 20   ☐ 21

Male :   ☐ 16   ☐ 17   ☐ 18   ☐ 19   ☐ 20   ☐ 21

Ethnic Group :   ☐ White   ☐ Asian   ☐ Chinese   ☐ other Black   ☐ other

Last permanent address

Tick if area of multiple deprivation :   ☐

Type of accommodation   ☐ parents   ☐ relatives   ☐ friends   ☐ B&B   ☐ other

Local connection   ☐ residency   ☐ work   ☐ other   ☐ none

Referral agency :   ☐ self   ☐ HD   ☐ SWD   ☐ CAB   ☐ other

Reasons for homelessness   ☐ evicted from family home   ☐ stepfamily problems

☐ parental violence   ☐ parental alcohol abuse

☐ sexual abuse   ☐ financial problems   ☐ other

Parents' marital status   ☐ married   ☐ separated   ☐ single/widowed

☐ reconstituted family

Where stayed since becoming homeless:

Experience of rooflessness   ☐ none   ☐ one   ☐ several

Social Work contact   ☐ none   ☐ previous   ☐ current

Experience of Residential Care   ☐ yes - where, how recent, how long?
☐ no

Police/Court involvement   ☐ none   ☐ pending   ☐ probation   ☐ CS   ☐ fine

Pregnancy   ☐ yes   ☐ no   ☐ not sure   ☐ not applicable

Other health problems:

Employment on entry   ☐ FT   ☐ PT   ☐ YTS   ☐ unemployed   ☐ FT education

Employment on leaving   ☐ FT   ☐ PT   ☐ YTS   ☐ unemployed   ☐ FT education

Length of stay at Project _____ weeks _____ days

Reason for leaving   ☐ 12 weeks up   ☐ return to family   ☐ found elsewhere

☐ project not right resource   ☐ discharged

Moving on address

Type of Accommodation   ☐ HD   ☐ HA   ☐ PRS   ☐ B&B   ☐ parents

☐ friends ☐ other_____

Housing Status   ☐ on priority list   ☐ appeal pending   ☐ no priority

CASE EXAMPLE 4
Monitoring use of a drop-in facility

Background and Reasons

Most projects providing direct care services keep comprehensive, accurate information, especially about those people using their core services. Less detailed information is usually noted about casual use of the service or people who contacted the project about other matters. As part of this research exercise, a few projects decided they would like more information about the number and type of people using part of their service on an unplanned, drop-in basis.

One example was a Family Centre based on a housing estate where many of the families in surrounding homes were experiencing social and economic difficulties. The core services of this project were group activities for children, young people, adults – for example, literacy skills classes – with an associated creche, a mothers and toddlers group and individual support and counselling for some people coming to these groups. Project workers found that many parents of children attending groups and parents using the adult groups or mother and toddler group dropped in at other times for advice, support or counselling or to chat about their child and/or practical matters. Children who lived nearby also called in before school and in the later afternoon.

The issues posed for staff were:

- having inadequate information about the level of this type of use of the project;
- demands on staff time and being diverted from other work;
- how to respond to the needs presented by the children and parents; and
- how to demonstrate this type of demand (and feedback from users) at a time when the future of the project was being reviewed.

What Was Done

The use made of the service on a drop-in basis was monitored over a two week period which was neither a particularly high or low period of activity. All staff, including the part-time administrative assistant and the cleaner, were to note everyone who came in on an unexpected basis. This therefore included people such as tradesmen and those coming in on a professional capacity who would not be regarded as users and who would then have to be sifted out at the analysis stage. However, it was decided to follow this approach as being easier to remember to record the information if there were no exceptions.

The project used a very simple layout on a A4 pad which was kept in a prominent place in the main office. The information sought was:-

- the date and a rough idea of the time;
- the name of the person who called;
- whether they were an existing user, or the parent of a child user;
- the reason/s for the person calling – for example, to use the phone, collect a child, ask advice, seek help in a crisis;
- what response the project staff gave – for example, give child breakfast, give advice, practical help, etc.

An example of the Record Sheet with fictitious details is:

Date: Monday 1 March

Caller	Client?	Reason	Response/Service
8.30 Mary Smith	Mother	Phone about break in	used phone advice, information support, tea
8.40 Helen, Joe Tracey	Yes	Chat breakfast note for school	listen, cuddles, milk, food washed children, wrote letter: follow up later

There were 4 steps in analysing the data:

1. The staff looked at patterns of use by specific people.

2. The sheets were marked and the information put into categories (see coding list below).

3. Lists of the frequency of types of callers, reasons and responses were drawn up.

4. Tables showing the reasons for different types of caller and the service given to different people were done.

Family Centre Drop-in: Coding Framework

Category of User:	child
	adult user
	parent/family member of user
	volunteer
	professionals: housing
	health
	police
	social work
	other
	other
Reasons:	advice, support
	1:1 work, counselling
	use resources
	use services
	play
	parenting-type care and support
	liaison, meeting
Response/service:	as for Reasons plus
	listening, social contact

Use of information

The intention was to analyse the information and use this in a report and for longer-term planning. The information gathered was analysed by the project leader using the simple coding/classification framework devised by the project leader and researcher. From this, the project established:

- the scale of use and peak times/days of drop-in activity;
- the balance between direct users, professionals, and others;

- which people were using the service in this way, whether they were recognised users or people who would not otherwise be identified as project users;
- the types of problems raised;
- whether people used an initial request – for example, about a practical matter – to raise other matters;
- responses by the project to different types of requests and issues.

The results from this exercise were used in a report for a review by the local authority, for planning within the project, and as a form of feedback from users: in this last respect, the results from this exercise were linked to those from a consumer feedback exercise.

Some of this information was acted upon very quickly by the project staff. In particular, the exercise made the project workers more aware of the way people used them and of the type of support they were providing in various situations. This was discussed within the project meeting, and although this matter had not arisen before the project workers very quickly reached a consensus view on how to respond and how services could be developed. The exercise also showed staff that a small number of people frequently – and intentionally – used the project in this way: this had not been readily apparent before because staff came in early or stayed on late in turns. The input offered by the project to these children and families was re-assessed and plans were made to address the underlying problems and/or offer a more intensive or different form of support.

Notes

The intention is to repeat this exercise three or four times during the year in order to establish patterns over the course of the year – such as seasonal demands – and year-to-year changes.

It was important that the recording of information did not disrupt the work of the project and was acceptable to staff and users. In practice, it was often not appropriate to record this information when the person was at the project, even though the level of information sought was minimal, because priority had to be given to dealing with the matter raised by the caller. However, project staff were confident that they did remember to record virtually every visit that happened within an hour or so of the event and that this information was accurate.

It was decided not to include people who came from groups and then sought staff out on another matter – for example, dropping in 10 minutes or so before

E

the group started or staying on at the end – although the exercise could have been expanded relatively easily to include these users.

Similar inputs and requests were recorded by different members of staff in slightly different ways. In this instance, this did not emerge as being a problem, partly because staff did discuss cases as they arose, which in turn led to a high level of consistency. The exercise as a whole and ways of describing common situations were also discussed by the staff team at the time of planning the exercise. For a larger staff group it would be important to take time to discuss in detail this type of exercise and how various situations would be recorded – perhaps taking a day or two as a trial run or pilot exercise.

One of the strengths of this approach is its flexibility. In this case the project wanted to look at the demands made by people not otherwise identified as users. This same basic method of recording events – using a simple notepad for a short period – can be used in other situations: for example, recording enquiries about places or referrals by other professionals, which is described in detail at Case Example 19. Here, the context of the columns and classification of information noted would change to reflect the issues which concerned the project.

This type of monitoring exercise is very useful as a one-off "snapshot" of a project's activities, or as a short survey which will be repeated every quarter or annually. It is less suitable as a method of on-going day-to-day recording of requests made by users: here, this approach could be used to establish the range of demands and could be followed up by the more structured approaches described for other models, where the analysis of the information would be more straight forward.

CASE EXAMPLE 5

Use of a drop-in facility: – survey of users

Background

The project in this Case Example was experiencing a similar problem to the Family Centre in the previous example, but took a different approach to tackling this.

This was a day care centre for older people. It was located in a community centre which had been purpose-built only a few years ago. The centre provided a range of activities for families living in the surrounding area. Most of the older people, however, lived very close to the centre – many of them within a few streets. The project encouraged its members to be as independent as possible and to use the centre as and when they wished. This was possible because physical access to the building was good. There were two entrances: one on the level and one with a gentle ramp and railings. Transport was provided by the centre for some of the most vulnerable users, but most people were able to make their way to the centre independently, walking or getting lifts from relatives, friends or volunteers.

As a result the use of the project was user-initiated to a larger extent than was usual for projects of this type. The project accepted referrals from home helps, GPs and other professionals, who usually suggested that a person come on a specified number of days per week. However some of these people tended to "pop in" for a chat or company at times other than 'their' days. It was also accepted that users could self-refer, and many people came along to the centre because a friend had started to come and had enjoyed it.

The project was keen to keep this flexibility, but was aware that some staff in the funding agencies (the local authority and the health board) would prefer a more conventional, structured approach. There were also concerns that the project was over-extending itself, although the Management Committee and staff were adamant that the levels and pattern of use made of the service were more stable than they might at first appear. However, the project did not routinely keep records about who attended when, other than to note the total numbers using the centre on any one day (for fire precaution and related purposes) and a number of meals which were taken (because they were funded separately for this).

They were therefore faced with the prospect of introducing a completely new monitoring system.

This project was also anxious to get feedback from their users about the facilities in the new centre and the way these were organised. The project had moved to the community centre from their own premises in a converted church hall about two years earlier. Although the new building was much more suitable in terms of physical access, warmer, brighter and safer, there had been a lot of critical comment about the loss of independence, having to share a building with other groups etc. In theory users now had access to a much wider range of activities, but staff were uncertain how far these were being taken up. Although the need for information about the way people were using the centre was pressing, staff put greater priority on the needs to get feedback from users. It was therefore decided to use the one approach – a survey of users – to answer both sets of information needs.

What Was Done

A survey of all the people who used the centre over a single week was carried out by volunteers. The time chosen was in the early autumn, when the summer holiday period was over and the absences from winter illnesses and bad weather had not yet begun. The users were kept informed about the plans for the survey through the monthly Members' Meeting and by large poster-type notices and leaflets. The decision to use volunteers was partly influenced by practicalities and partly by the aim of having as unbiased feedback as possible. The paid and volunteer staff who worked at the day centre were already fully-committed, and did not want to disrupt their usual work with users to distribute and collect forms. They also thought it more likely that users would be honest in their comments and make criticisms where appropriate if these were being dealt with by someone else. The people who were roped into help, however, were mostly known to at least some of the users through activities run by local churches and other voluntary projects, some members of the Management Committee and similar "friends and hangers-on".

On the Monday of "survey week" volunteers were at the centre to distribute and gather back in the forms. If the member wished to complete the form herself she was left to do this. However the volunteers helped some members, for example those with limited hand movement following a stroke or with poor sight. This was done in a gentle, non-stigmatising way – "shall I do the writing while you do the thinking?" There were also instances of one member noting down comments for a friend.

The form that was used was essentially in two parts. The top part noted which days the person came to the centre. The plan was that everyone would fill in the first part on each day that they came during the week. In practice, however, the volunteers simply marked off the days on subsequent visits for some users, especially those who were confused, found communication difficult or would have been upset by the repeated requests.

The second and larger part of the form was the survey, asking people their views on the service and ideas for new activities, what activities they currently used. This survey was filled out only on the first occasion somebody used the centre. Perhaps inevitably, a few people filled in this part of the form on subsequent visits, and one of the tasks of the volunteers was to sift out these duplicate returns.

Analysis and Use of the Information

The centre coordinator and a couple of the volunteers who had helped carry out the survey took responsibility for analysing the returned forms. This was a large day centre with around 200 people using it over the week, which was around 90% of the people currently on the centre's membership list. The number of days each person attended was checked and marked on the completed survey form. They then counted the number of people who had come once, twice per week etc. This was linked to the question on the survey about how frequently people came to the centre. This information was spread back to the funders at the next Advisory Group meeting.

The information from the rest of the survey was analysed over the course of several afternoons spread over the next month or so. Since the project does not have a computer this had to be done manually, along the lines described in Part 3 of this handbook. This information was fed back to the users, through the same channels as the original consultation, and to the Advisory Group. The project also drew on this in their annual report.

The project staff and Management Committee later spent some time considering their arrangements for monitoring the way in which members used their project. It was agreed that it would be useful to repeat this snapshot review every so often, for example to see if there was a difference in the pattern of use at the height of the winter. They also decided to introduce a system whereby each member of staff had responsibility for a list of members, and had to note each week whether or not the person had been in. However they confirmed their earlier decision not to introduce a very detailed monitoring system which recorded each person's daily use of the project. These arrangements were discussed with the funders and it was agreed to try these compromise arrangements for the year and then review it.

CASE EXAMPLE 6

Monitoring service to individual users

Background

This example is drawn from another day care centre for older people, but this time offering a very different type of service. This project gave very tailored packages of care to individual users, and as a result the levels and type of care given to different people varied widely, reflecting the users' needs and wishes. The project provided personal care such as bathing, and was the base for chiropody and community nursing care. The project also provided outreach/befriending services, which again covered a range of activities such as exchanging library books, shopping, spending afternoons with the older people etc. There was a support group for carers, most of whom had relatives at the day care centre, and the outreach service sometimes provided respite to allow carers to come to this group. However these two additional services were organised separately from the main day centre activities by different people, and involved a different group of volunteers.

There was a very detailed set of records for each person at the time of the original referral. Changes in members' home circumstances and the levels of care provided by other services were noted as necessary, and the project staff were confident that they knew what was happening to their users outwith the centre. However they probably knew less about how people received services within the project. Each individual service or part of the centre had its own records – for the befriending scheme, carer support, the bathing book, lists for the different social activities. The staff felt that their flexible approach was beginning to get a bit unwieldy. They were anxious that some people could be benefiting from a different combination of services and that the quality of service would be better if the different inputs were better coordinated. In practice people at the centre did keep each other well informed about individual users, but as the coordinator put it they were "missing the big picture".

What Was Done

The project drew up a very simple record sheet for each person who was currently on their list of users. This was done by the coordinator for the main day centre and by the volunteer or other worker who organised the different inputs. Even just checking off the names on the different lists was a useful exercise. A record sheet was drawn up for every user, with separate copies for the befriending volunteers to take with them. The main copies were kept in the office and over the course of a week everyone noted what they did with or for that user or the person's carer.

The sheets were then analysed by the coordinator and the secretary. From this they were able to work out what range of services each individual user was receiving. Where there was some gaps – for example when a carer might benefit from the support group but wasn't in touch with them, someone would arrange to follow this up and suggest this to the member or carer.

They also identified how often people were using the different services, for example the number of users who were in touch with the befriending scheme once/twice etc during the week, the number of people who received some form of personal or nursing care once/twice etc and those involved in the various social activities.

3

What difference have we made? Identifying the outcomes of services

IMPORTANCE OF IDENTIFYING OUTCOMES

Once we have established how a service is being used, the next thing to consider is what difference this makes to the people concerned. Voluntary organisations and other agencies provide services in order that something will happen – people will learn something, enjoy themselves, circumstances will change for the better, something unpleasant will be stopped or reduced. There has sometimes been a tendency to simply assume that all these changes actually happen, without ever checking out that this was so. It is also sometimes assumed that everybody benefits in much the same way or has the same sort of outcomes, and because of this important changes sometimes go unrecognised.

Establishing the outcomes of services is an important way of identifying the quality of services. Indeed many voluntary organisations say that this is what makes them special or different – that they achieve different things from similar services, or tackle needs that would otherwise get missed.

As the section explaining Monitoring and Evaluation in the first part of the handbook showed, it is also important to understand the links between what a project puts into an activity and what users and other people get out of it. Which things do you do that make the biggest difference? How did your service tackle users' needs? This is important for all voluntary organisations, but especially for those providing community care services for elderly and other vulnerable people where the projects may have to explain how they contribute to packages of care involving other services.

Considering the outcomes of services is something that rarely happens as a separate activity. Instead, it is usually a strong feature of information systems which bring together material on how people come to use the project and how users and others view their experience of the project and the changes it makes. This therefore overlaps with establishing the scale and pattern of use and with consumer and agency feedback.

The outcomes of services can be established at 2 levels:

- **the individual case,** when the project is planning how to give the best possible service to that particular person; and
- **for the project overall.**

Outcomes can best be identified for individual people. The starting point is to note the objectives and expectations of the user, referer and other relevant people, and then looking at whether these have been met, again taking account of the views of the people concerned. This can then be used to provide feedback or planning at case level – for example individual case planning, case conferences etc. This is also the basis for considering the outcomes of service overall – for example, comparing what has happened to different groups of people, such as those who had received only the main service and those who had also received additional services, or the outcome for people in different situations. The difference between considering outcomes at case and project levels lies in how the information is used and analysed, rather than the basic approach to gathering and recording it.

PARTICULAR ISSUES

Before getting involved in this type of work, it needs to be recognised that identifying outcomes is more complicated than other aspects of the monitoring and evaluation work which projects are being expected or encouraged to undertake. There are certain points that you will need to take account of.

The first problem associated with describing outcomes is that no one can be absolutely certain that one particular thing – in this case the project's services – actually *caused* another – the changes that happen to users. While the project is providing its services lots of other things will be happening in the lives of its users. For example, everyone might agree that a frail older lady is now more settled and happier than she was when she first came to the day centre six months ago. However, this could be as much because her family has moved closer, or she has got a cat, as it is because of the practical help and support she is getting at the day centre. The likely explanation is that it is a combination of things, which are often reinforcing and supporting each other if they are all working to the good, or offsetting other changes if the experience is bad or mixed.

What this means is that a project cannot claim that it and it alone caused the outcomes which are identified for its users. It can however say that these outcomes happened, and that these were associated with people's use of the service.

Some changes that happen for people are quite small or are hard to pin down. When a care and repair scheme fixes someone's roof and the water stops coming in we know it has happened. On the other hand, changes like gaining company, friendship, greater self confidence and the like are much harder to define. However, they are just as real and important to the people concerned and are the kinds of things which the users themselves may note as being very important. (See for example Case Example 9 in the user feedback section.)

The timescale over which any outcomes are measured is another problem. Sometimes projects are dealing with fairly short timescales, such as a few months, while others are trying to make changes that will effect people over many years to come. When starting out identifying the outcome of services you need to think about what is an appropriate timescale. People's circumstances are changing all the time, so the longer the span the more scope there is for all these other things to happen to them, along the lines of the problems discussed above. You need to be clear what time periods you are taking as your start and finish points and be careful to use similar periods for everyone if you are going to talk about another group, or else make clear that outcomes are being measured over a different timescale. Case Example 9 in the user feedback section looked at what had happened to a group of people over the past year and did not try to go any further back than this.

You also need to decide how wide you are going to take the outcomes. Are you concerned with just what has happened to the main user, or also to their carer and family? Are you interested in the way people use other services and what has then happened to the other services? Are you only interested in their connection other services have with that client, or are you interested in what happened when they were able to offer a place to someone else after you took on a referral from them?

For many projects in this fieldwork, which were giving fairly intensive services, all these points were relevant and were covered when the outcomes of services were addressed. However, this will not always be the case. For example, an advice and information service, or an outdoor activity service for school children, will mostly focus just on the individual users themselves.

HOW TO IDENTIFY OUTCOMES

A classic research approach to these problems in identifying outcomes is to have a control group. This is when there are two groups of people in the same circumstances. One group receives the service or has something happen to them, while the other one doesn't. You then compare what happens to the two groups.

If everything else is the same, it can be assumed that the service or treatment or whatever is associated with any differences in the outcomes for the two groups.

There are some problems associated with this, however. The first is that it is generally not considered right to refuse someone a service just to have a neat comparison. There are sometimes situations though when this is not a problem – for example, you could compare what happens to people on your waiting list to those who are getting the service.

At first glance another option might be that the people who are getting other services from other providers or living in another area where your service is not available. However these are generally not good comparisons for the people getting the service that we want to examine. These other groups of people are unlikely to be in exactly the same circumstances as the group who are using your project. In the same way, to go back to the comparison between your waiting list and existing services, you would need to check whether there were other factors such as people on the waiting list getting other services in the meantime, or whether you always give priority to most needy cases, which would mean the two groups were not exactly the same.

Comparisons are useful but have to be done carefully. If you do want to draw comparisons between what has happened to people using your project and another group, it is a good idea to talk this over with someone. If you have access to an experienced researcher this is a good time to use them. Another useful person to check your plans with is someone from the other agencies with which you work, to see if they also think the comparison is a sensible one.

There are also well-established ways of making an independent assessment of the outcome in all cases against some consistent measurements. Sometimes there is a recognised way of describing or charting what happens to people that is relevant to your projects and is also simple to use. An example is the number of people learning a sport or musical instrument who pass a particular exam or reach a certain standard. If there is a yardstick of this sort then it can be very helpful. A lot depends on how complicated the measurements are and whether they would be used anyway. This approach was used by a few projects in the fieldwork who were noting children's progress against standard assessments used by teachers and other experts. A few other projects in the fieldwork tried to measure outcomes against complicated assessments. The view taken by all the people concerned is that it took a lot of work and the benefits to the project and the quality of information gained as a result were no better than that gained by simpler methods. Using some standard yardstick is a good idea if it is simple and helps you in your work with individual people. It is probably not worth using if it is complicated and just for the monitoring and evaluation of the project overall: again if you do want to do this it is best to get advice from an experienced researcher.

Another well-established approach is to base assessments of outcomes on the judgement of experienced people who know the circumstances of the people concerned and know the service network in that area. This has been found by other research studies to be a reliable test of what the changes are to users and to what would probably have happened to them if the project hadn't been there. This is especially useful when you are trying to measure this preventative aspect of service delivery. This judgement can be built on and is the basis of the approach that is used in Case Example 7 of this guide. Another important element of Case Example 7 and especially of Case Example 8 is checking out with the users what they think had changed and what they think would have happened if the centre had not been there. In both these examples any assessment of outcome is based on the view of several people. This has the great advantage of avoiding relying on only one person's view.

WHAT WAS DONE

Half the 26 projects in the fieldwork for this research study included a specific examination of the outcomes of services they provided as part of the monitoring and evaluation work. Despite there being a wide range of projects providing care to children and families in different settings and different types of day care centres working for older people, two basic methods were used for addressing outcomes of services. Technically, these were both very simple.

The first method was a simple index-card system, where the project staff noted the user's circumstances, reasons for using the service, the service input and then the outcomes of the person, other family members and other agencies. This is explained in Case Example 7.

The second method was a summary sheet which was used as part of existing case record systems. It complemented the other sources of information and brought together the viewpoints of the various people involved. Again, this built on the idea of starting off with noting what the project was trying to achieve and then looking at what later happened. However, this introduced a greater degree of structure, and so is particularly useful where a high level of consistency is needed. This is illustrated in Case Example 8.

CASE EXAMPLE 7

Review of users' circumstances and outcome

Need for Information

Many direct service providers know a great deal about their users – their circumstances, the way in which they use the project and other services and the benefits gained and other outcomes for the users themselves, their carers or families and staff in other services. This is not always recorded in a way that is easily accessible or that can provide an overview of how all users are getting on. Some information may be noted in a range of places – referral forms, records for specific services such as transport lists, membership of groups meeting on different days, notes on (some) individual users' files. A lot of information will be personal to staff – such as informal conversations with users, their relatives or other professionals – and is not recorded anywhere.

Several projects in the fieldwork for the research study identified this as a problem. Some specific issues which they raised were:

- the need to have a reliable system for reviewing the care given to individual users – for example, whether the user was still getting the most appropriate service in the light of changing needs – and for feeding in to multi-agency case reviews;
- the need to establish that the project had contributed to positive outcomes for the users (for example, helping prevent admission to respite or hospital care, helping a teenager settle back into school, easier relationships between family members) by something stronger than anecdotes;
- what to do about information known to staff ("stored in our heads"), especially when there was a high turnover of volunteers/staff after a long period of stability; and
- finding an informal, accessible way of putting information together which would not put heavy demands on staff time and could even save time by minimising repetition.

The Projects

These issues were raised by staff in day care centres and in children and families projects working in a variety of ways. Common features were fairly large numbers of users and a fluctuating staff group – for example, frequent use of volunteers, students and short-term employment.

The first example is a day care centre for vulnerable older people based in a county town serving it and the local area. It aimed to help users remain in their own homes or with their families by giving a fairly intensive service. The centre is open every weekday and a few people come in every day although most attend on two or three specified days. The project linked in to other services and checked which services users were receiving at the time of referral, although this was not always updated.

The project had a fairly good ratio of staff (mostly volunteers) to users: since they spent a considerable amount of time talking and listening to users and had frequent contact with carers who lived with their elderly parent or nearby they felt they knew what was happening in users' lives and were confident the centre was providing important benefits. However, there were no case records on individual users. Recent requests to feed into case conferences about a few users had put a lot of stress on the project in terms of putting together notes and trying recall when changes happened. The staff and committee hoped to participate in planning care and services for other users in future, but needed some kind of record system for this. At the same time they wanted to check whether they were still giving an appropriate service, especially to members who had been using the service for many years – 10 and more in some cases.

The second example is a youth project working with young people aged 12 to 16 who were having difficulties settling at school, were in trouble with the police (eg petty shoplifting) and/or had problems at home. The project worked with them on a group-work basis and provided one-to-one counselling and befriending support. Some groups were activity-based while others focused on specific issues. Whereas most children were referred for a specific reason – often by the Reporter or Children's Panel on a compulsory basis – a few were self-selected when someone asked to bring along a friend or sibling. In addition the project ran a summer playscheme and an after-school story-time club once a week for younger children in a conscious attempt to avoid the project being thought of as only for "problem teenagers".

This project had very good case records on all referred children, including a review system which included feedback and comments from the young person and his parent/s. Basic information was held on the "extra" children but the benefits which they gained were not formally noted as they did not represent the project's and other professionals' main priority. Over time, project staff had become aware that the circumstances and needs of these "extra" children were becoming closer to their main caseload. They were concerned that the project was not addressing these children's needs, but were also concerned about potential implications for the project's service to their main users if the input to these children was stepped up with no extra resources. For the children attending the main groups, the project was planning to review how these were organised and wanted to compare success of cases where children also received additional inputs.

What was done

The system devised to identify the outcomes for people using these projects was a fairly simple one. It summarised information already available to the project or possibly stored in greater detail elsewhere. It brought together three main areas:

- the user's characteristics and circumstances;
- the input of the project to that person or family;
- the outcomes for the user, carers/family and other agencies.

An outline of the main headings and type of information noted for two projects is attached.

Both projects adapted the list of headings to suit their circumstances. The day care centre wanted a more detailed section on the circumstances of the user, noting circumstances of carers as a separate item and having a lengthy checklist for other services. Otherwise, the structure was the same.

Both projects recorded the information on index cards, noting the main points and trying to use key words as far as possible. An example of the layout used is also attached at the end of the Case Example. It would also be possible to use A4 sheets if it was more convenient or if more detailed information was wanted, or to use a data-base on the computer if this was available. The information was analysed by counting how many people had the main characteristics (for example, the numbers of men and women, number of elderly people living alone, number of children excluded from school, number with home problems); how many were using particular services (home help, remedial teaching); and how many received the main types of benefits. This was done by simply counting the cards where the relevant characteristic or outcome was noted. This was followed by a more complex analysis, mostly of the outcomes for people in different circumstances or receiving different types of input. This was done by separating out the cards where the relevant feature was noted and then counting the other factors in the same way as before for each bundle.

The youth project spread the task of completing the cards between several members of staff, with each person taking responsibility for groups of users where they were the key worker. The project discussed what the main points of relevant information were and agreed what they recognised as specific benefits. This meant there was a fairly high level of consistency in the terms used and the way similar items were recorded from the outset. The coordinator then discussed the completed cards with staff, which provided a further level of checking. The completion of cards for the referred users was straightforward: information was already to hand but had to be summarised and updated. As expected, however, less information was available for the other children: more time was needed for that and it was decided to accept that some information was not available.

The coordinator and part-time administrator/secretary at the day care centre pulled together information already available on about a third of users, then added to this by checking with other staff and the health visitor who sat on the management committee. The project then repeated this for another set of users, and so on. Those users in the first set included those who were most likely to be involved in a case conference or similar change in their circumstances, and therefore comprised the most vulnerable users – in other words, the cases where the information was likely to be needed soonest. This in itself was a helpful stage as, in the course of discussing who this definition included, the coordinator, health visitor and a few experienced volunteers defined their understanding of risks and relevant personal and home circumstances. This made completing the cards much more straightforward. This project was not under any acute time pressures and, in all, it took about five months for all the basic information to be gathered, while the analysis stage took another three months or so.

How the Findings were Used

Both projects produced reports covering the breakdown of circumstances of people using the service, the number getting additional support, and types of benefits gained by people in different circumstances. They also used the information to assess their services.

The youth project submitted this to the local authority and this was part of the basis for discussions about the type of service the project should be delivering: as a result they have decided to refocus some activities. One of the points identified by this review was that the circumstances of the "extra" children were broadly similar to the referred users although their problems were mostly less extreme. The types of benefits gained by children attending the same activity groups were also broadly similar: an increase in self confidence and learning new skills tended to be noted for all children, although an improvement in school work was more noticeable among the referred children, who tended to have greater problems here. One of the points which the project decided to follow up after this exercise was to establish more contact with the children's families outwith the formal review system.

The day care centre discussed the paper within their committee and agreed they did not want to change anything to the overall services. This project used the information for several case conferences over the next few months, where the coordinator felt more confident about stating her views based on the project's contact with the older person. The centre then attached the report to their next application for annual funding.

Both projects have decided to review services on an annual basis. The day care centre is effectively using this to review the care given to individual users: the coordinator, health visitor and a volunteer look at some cases every month, updating information on the card. This project does not expect to do another overview, but feel confident that they could do this quite easily if it was ever needed. The youth project, on the other hand, is planning to repeat the overall analysis of activities and outcomes as part of a review of the new arrangements once these have been running for about a year.

Notes

This general approach has also been used by other services. Descriptions of how ideas similar to this have been used by two day care centres are given in the Age Concern publication at Case Examples two and five.

From the experience of these two projects and others which have used this approach, some key steps have been identified to setting the system up.

- It is helpful to discuss and agree relevant points of information, definitions of risk and benefits and similar matters before launching into recording information. The lists attached at the end of this case example can form the basis of this, but need to reflect the circumstances of each particular project.

- When gathering information for all existing users it is helpful to start noting what is already available and, where appropriate, then check this out and check other points with the user and other people and update earlier information. This takes time to do properly, but can be spread out round several people or the entire task broken up and done in stages.

- The recording of information for the review should be kept simple and short: remember that this is not designed to replace other detailed records where these are needed.

- Once the system is up and running similar arrangements are needed to keep it up to date – for example by adding cards for new users or a periodic review of cases. Again, responsibility for this can lie with one person or be spread around, but this needs to be agreed and understood.

REVIEW OF USERS' CIRCUMSTANCES AND OUTCOMES OF SERVICES: YOUTH PROJECTS

1. *Circumstances of User*

   - age, personality, health
   - family, [problems experienced by family if relevant]
   - use of other agencies: School, other Education Department inputs, Social Work Department, health services, Reporters or Children's Panel
   - any statutory orders
   - risk [for example of personal harm, increased statutory involvement, exclusion from other services]

2. *Why User came to this Group*

   - how/by whom young person was referred
   - what that person and other people hoped or expected s/he would get out of project

3. *Use of the Project*

   - this group: frequency, activities, participation
   - other elements of the project
   - length of time with Project [if appropriate to project]
   - other inputs from project or other parts of organisation [if relevant]

4. *Benefits and other Outcomes for User*

   - skills, experience
   - personal relationships, friendships
   - relationships within family
   - school work
   - changes in relevant specific behaviour [such as offending, truanting]
   - use of other services
   - whether any risk aspects have changed

5.   *Benefits/Outcomes for other members of the family*

- relationships within family
- ability to cope with young person's behaviour
- parents' own health
- access to other services

6.   *Benefits/Outcomes for other services*

- supplementing input of other services
- reinforcing situation for other professionals
- casefinding
- contributing to service planning, such as information fed in to reviews

REVIEW OF USERS' CIRCUMSTANCES AND OUTCOMES OF SERVICES: DAY CARE PROJECTS FOR OLDER PEOPLE

1.   *Circumstances of User*

- age, gender
- health: general health; handicaps; mobility problems; sensory handicaps
- mental health, confused – dementia diagnosed?; depression; learning difficulty; other aspects
- personal care: incontinence problems; bathing etc
- social integration

2.   *Characteristics of Family, Carers*

- are there any carers nearby?
- involvement of extended family, neighbours, friends
- stresses on carers and others
- relevant personal circumstances of carers, such as ill-health, other responsibilities

3.   *Use of Other Services*

Checklist covering Social Work Department, Health Service and other voluntary inputs available in that area.

4. *Overall Risk**

- of personal harm
- community support breaking down
- exclusion from other services

*Framework for assessing level of coping/risk used by a few projects attached.

5. *Why User came to this Project*

- how/by whom person was referred or heard of project
- what that person and other people hoped or expected she/he would get out of project

6. *Use of the Project*

- this day care service: frequency, activities, participation
- length of time with Project
- use of other elements of the project or Organisation's service [if relevant]

7. *Benefits and other Outcomes for User*

- happier, less anxious
- personal development, confidence
- personal relationships, friendships
- relationships with family
- able to stay in own home
- use of other services
- whether any risk aspects identified have changed

8. *Benefits/Outcomes for other members of the family*

- able to do other things: for example go on holiday, stay in employment
- have respite breaks
- obtained or easier access to other services
- own health improved or not deteriorating
- relationships with family easier
- ability to accept or cope with situation enhanced
- better able to continue to provide care.

9. *Benefits/Outcomes for other services*

- releasing places in other services for other people
- reinforcing other work, for example reminding person to take medicine
- monitoring situation for them
- casefinding – identifying people who have slipped through the service net
- contributing to planning services, such as information fed in to reviews.

FRAMEWORK FOR ASSESSING COPING OR RISK

Coping Well/Low Risk

Person and/or carers are coping as well as could be expected and this is expected to continue.

There is no risk to the person's well-being.

Typical features are:

- person may be too ill/frail/confused, but their condition is stable or controlled;
- the person is alert and motivated enough to cope;
- there is good support from the person's family and extended informal network and from services, with back-ups readily available;
- the person is coping on most aspects of day-to-day living or has good help and advice.

Barely Coping/Medium Risk

The person and her carers are coping at present, but are unlikely to cope with an increased demand.

There is no risk to the person's physical well-being yet, but this is possible in the foreseeable future.

Typical features are:

- the person's physical and/or mental health is deteriorating;
- care demands are high and continuous;
- the carer's ability to cope has been reduced, for example through ill-health or other commitments;
- there is some behaviour which is risky and/or problems in managing own affairs, but this is monitored and/or infrequent.

Not Coping/High Risk

Person is wholly dependent on services or carers and would not cope with any reduction in current level, even for a short while.

Person's physical well-being is at risk.

Carers are under great pressure.

Situation is likely to break down.

Typical features are:

- self-neglect, such as not eating, poor personal care;
- risk of abuse from others;
- person's own behaviour is putting them at risk, for example unreliable use of medication, wandering at night;
- not managing day-to-day affairs such as paying bills;
- person's condition is unstable or is likely to deteriorate and needs constant monitoring;
- project is essential (along with input from other services) to maintain person safely in the community.

CASE EXAMPLE 8
Standard review form

Background and Reasons

In many projects offering direct care there are planned reviews of the user's circumstances and progress made by the project and person, usually at planned intervals throughout the user's time with the project and at the close of the case. This pattern is likely to become even more common with the greater emphasis on case conferences and care assessment and planning under the new Community Care arrangements.

Because these reviews focus on issues relevant to that particular person's circumstances and the meetings are recorded by different members of staff in slightly different ways, it is often difficult to bring these together to draw out common issues and outcomes for the group of users. On the other hand, it is usually a good idea to minimise changes to the way staff carry out and record these reviews if this already works well for the individual cases.

Several projects decided to tackle this by introducing a standard sheet which summarised the main points from the individual records and set these out in a form which could be read and analysed easily.

The Project

The example given here comes from a project providing an alternative to custody in prison for young people aged 16-21 who have been convicted of an offence. The main focus of the project is on the person's offending behaviour, but the factors associated with this and the consequences for the person are also addressed in most cases, and the most frequently raised points are listed on the second page of the record sheet. The service is usually provided for twelve weeks on the basis of a contract between the project and the user, although there may be some continuing contact over the next few months.

The intention was to use these standard review forms as a 'progress checklist' for each case, as the objectives and outcomes agreed at interim reviews are carried on to the next stage of the project's work with the user. The project and user could agree to focus on a particular factor which had contributed to the person getting into trouble – for example a drink problem – or a problem caused by or linked to his recent behaviour – such as family relationships breaking up. The record system then provided a way of assessing what progress had been made by the time of the next review.

The record sheets also provided a way of looking across all the current or previous users and identifying patterns and circumstances common to the cases.

When all the forms were taken together they formed the basis for reports on the qualitative aspects of the project's work. Examples of this included the proportions of young people for whom particular factors had contributed to getting into trouble, the characteristics of the group, the levels of success achieved by the project in tackling particular issues and the outcomes for the users receiving different types of services from the project. This was used by the project and the Management Committee to plan services and for other purposes, for example in annual reports to the funders and other services with which the project worked.

Notes

The main purpose of this system is to provide a convenient way of tracking and recording outcomes for the user. However, it is also useful in summarising and collating information on

- the *pattern of use*; the **Work Done** column of the **Objectives agreed with the user** and any input from the project at **Continuing work**, and
- relevant *characteristics of the user*; here, the key points of the person's offending history noted under **Referral**.

Standard review sheets like this are intended to complement other record-keeping systems, rather than stand alone. As well as the detailed case notes on the reviews mentioned, the project in this example also kept a referral book, which noted users' personal characteristics and other information, and has copies of the contract agreed with each user.

Information systems like this can also draw together information on what happened to people using several projects. The voluntary organisation in this Case Example is presently negotiating with several other local authorities to set up similar services. When these become active it will be possible to amend these forms to identify the project, thus providing managers with an overview of the issues being raised and tackled and of qualitative outcomes.

Another way this approach might be used would be to form a common basis for a range of services meeting needs of a single client group, such as home supports, day care and short-term respite projects working with elderly, ill or disabled people.

ALTERNATIVES TO CUSTODY: REVIEW FORM

☐ mid-way ☐ closing

Name: Age:

Key worker: Case Ref:

Referral

source: offence/s:

main reasons: court:

                             previous history:

Objectives agreed with User

	List	Work Done	Progress/Outcome to date
1.			
2.			
3.			
4.			
5.			

Key Outcomes, Notes

Present Circumstances, Changes

Offending Behaviour

Personal Relationships
- family

- peer group

Perception of Self

Accommodation

Alcohol, etc.

Employment, Training, Education

Leisure Time

Use of other services

Continuing Work
Project: Other Agencies:

User:

4
Feedback from users

The importance of getting feedback from users is now being given a lot more attention than before – for example, having a system for obtaining user feedback is usually now a condition of grant. This also reflects increased emphasis on good practice: knowing what our users think about services is an essential step to ensuring that we give good quality services that are useful and helpful to the people concerned.

Getting feedback from the people who used the services was covered by 14 of the 26 projects in the study. Most of the other schemes already had good feedback arrangements. This was the aspect of this monitoring and evaluation work which the project staff thought was the most important. They wanted to learn what people thought about the project, which aspects they liked and disliked and what they wanted changed. They wanted to hear what had happened to people and how the users and their families or carers saw their current situation. This was the element which project staff found most enjoyable. It was also perhaps the most thought-provoking: asking people what they think can mean hearing a few surprises and having to re-think your plans.

Many different types of people use social care and other voluntary projects. Their circumstances will affect the way in which we gather their views and ideas. Projects sought feedback from children, teenagers, young adults, parents, people with learning difficulties and older people, some of whom had senile dementia. These users included people who had characteristics commonly associated with factors which make feedback of this sort more difficult.

- **Limited verbal or written communication skills:** some of the younger children had only just started school; some adults had limited literacy skills; some older people found speech or writing difficult following a stroke or another illness.
- **Language:** all of the people from ethnic minority communities in the user feedback exercises had good spoken English, but users in other fieldwork projects did not speak English.

- **Limited understanding of the issues:** at first sight this affected the children, people with learning disabilities and older people with dementia.

- **Confidentiality on sensitive issues:** even though the users of these projects were in contact with staff on a range of personal matters some people clearly preferred to keep some aspects of their lives private, while some topics were potentially embarrassing, such as criticising a service they would have to go on using.

- **Apprehension about questions:** some people were expected to feel uncomfortable about being asked questions on personal matters, for example when they had been subject to a long series of assessments and interviews or this was associated with unpleasant consequences such as a reduction in income.

In all these circumstances it was possible to find a way of obtaining reliable feedback. This was partly a matter of using the right method of gathering information in these circumstances. It was also partly about having the right attitude and project staff using their imagination and ingenuity, as some of the Case Examples in this handbook and the Age Concern booklet illustrate. The key is to think about how to go about getting this information from the point of view of the users, rather than of the people providing the service. A useful account of getting feedback from users – in this case people with learning disabilities – is the evaluation of the Putting People First project (details are in the book list in the last section). This explains how the whole approach was centred on the users – from influencing which topics were covered in the evaluation to the phasing of the questions and means of responding (for example using cards with happy and sad faces rather than very good/good/poor etc).

Methods of gathering information used by the projects in this study included:

- the usual questionnaires, where the person fills in the information and returns the completed form;

- spoken questionnaires; where someone asks the user the question and notes the answer;

- research interviews, where an outsider interviews the user in confidence: the project later received the overall results but not details of individual cases;

- group discussions, where a group of users and perhaps volunteers or staff discussed the questions and give a combined response; and

- incorporating feedback questions into the ongoing casework and discussion with users, rather than having it as a separate contact.

The table on page 84 shows which methods have been found most useful in particular circumstances. The Case Examples describe ways in which these methods were used. These also illustrate how it can sometimes be a good idea to use more than one method to deal with the circumstances of that project and its users.

Other ways of making feedback easier for users include:

- keeping the questions and the language as simple as possible;

- using "tick-box" type questions instead of only "please write in" ones;

- allowing people to give anonymous answers;

- giving users the choice to write in their own answers or have someone do this for them;

- letting users choose who will record answers on their behalf (in a group discussion among 5-8 year olds the "big ones" wrote the comments on behalf of the group. The language was simple and there were spelling mistakes, but the views expressed were very clear and on some points quite sophisticated);

- making the collection points for returned survey forms visible, accessible and appropriate ("Please give this to any volunteer in a yellow T-shirt" or "return to Mary or Jim" rather than "leave on the desk".);

- having someone go to collect replies rather than leaving this to the user.

Making things easier for the user is also of help to the project. People are more likely to make a response and to give more accurate and more useful information if the experience is easy than if it is difficult and complicated.

SUMMARY OF METHODS OF GATHERING USER FEEDBACK IN DIFFERENT CIRCUMSTANCES

Circumstances	Method				
	Written Questionnaire	Oral Questionnaire	Interview	Group Discussion	Casework
Number of people involved - large	*	P	-	P (series)	P
Number of people involved - small	*	*	*	P	*
Limited time available	P	P	-	*	-
Limited resources	*	-	-	*	-
Dispersed target population	*	-	P (telephone)	-	*
communication skills limited	-	*	*	P	-
Need to identify broad range of views	P	P	-	*	-
Need to get complete and/or very accurate response	-	P	*	-	-
Want respondents to reflect on circumstances, changes; to discuss feelings or views	P	*	*	-	*
Consumers suspicious of outsiders or of questioning	-	*	- (project staff)	*	*

*: suitable

P: possible - more suitable in some circumstances or for some groups of people, not suitable for others

-: not suitable or needs extra skill or experiencete

84

CASE EXAMPLE 9

Survey of users' views: questionnaire

Background and Circumstances

As the table in the introduction to this section showed, giving people a written list of questions can be used in a wide range of circumstances. It is probably the first method we think of when finding out people's views is suggested.

Its main advantages are that the users can complete the answers in their own time and it can be made anonymous. For the staff, the time spent in preparing and then giving out a form to 100 people – perhaps spread over a wide area – is usually not much greater than giving it to 10 people, while if the form is well-designed the time needed to draw together and make sense of the answers can also be kept to a minimum.

The main disadvantages are that it is less easy to make allowances for cases which are very different from the others, and it can sometimes be hard work to get the users to give back the completed forms.

This way of gathering feedback from users is probably best when:

- the users will be in broadly similar circumstances to each other, at least as far as their use of the project is concerned;
- there is a reasonable-sized group of people involved: if it is less than 10 or so you may be as well asking people the questions personally;
- you are fairly confident of getting a good number of replies, or can find ways of encouraging people to reply promptly;
- you have enough time to wait for the forms to be copied, given or posted out, returned and then read and analysed.

The Project

This example is drawn from a youth project based in a rural area, working with young people aged 12 to 15 who are having difficulties coping at school or home or who have been in trouble. Like many other focused services of this sort, the project runs a review system at which the young people and their parents are involved. However this concentrated on aspects of each child's and family's circumstances at that time and did not seek to take a longer-term or wider view.

This project had been running for several years and was due to have its funding and structure reviewed by the local authority. It was decided by the Project

Management Committee and staff to bring together the views of users. This would feed into the coming review and would help the project to plan future services. A survey of professionals in various agencies with whom the project worked was also carried out at the same time.

What Was Done

A small working group of the co-ordinator, line manager and a few members of the Committee was formed to run this exercise. Over two meetings they pulled together a list of topics which were then refined to actual questions. At this stage they checked that similar or equivalent questions were being asked of both parents and young people when appropriate, so that they had different points of view on the same issues.

The survey was to be given to all children who had used the project within the previous year, to give some time for initial feelings and changes to settle down. The survey was done over the summer holidays when there were few current services and the people planning and doing the survey were (slightly) less busy. Given the numbers involved (40 young people and their parents) and geographic spread it was decided to use questionnaires rather than other forms of information gathering such as group discussions or interviews.

Once the list of questions was available this was given to a few children currently using the scheme who would not be included in the main survey. They were asked to fill in the forms as a "pilot" and some questions were reworded to take account of their comments. Similarly, a few parents who had used the project a few years previously but who still had contact with the project or a Committee Member were asked to pilot the parents' questionnaire.

Copies of the final version were posted out with a covering letter from the Chair of the Management Committee. A pre-paid envelope was also included. Around half the families replied within a few weeks. Repeat questionnaires were sent out two weeks after the first letter, with a letter thanking all those who had replied and encouraging/reminding others. This brought the total response rate up to around 70%, which would be considered satisfactory for most surveys of this type.

At this point they departed from the traditional postal survey approach. The Steering Group were keen to improve this response if at all possible. A Committee Member volunteered to deliver a fresh copy of the questionnaire to those people who had still not responded. In about half the cases this offer to come back and collect the forms in a day or so was sufficient to secure a response. She then helped many of the dozen or so remaining respondents – both children and parents – to complete the questionnaire in the way described in the next case example. This brought the total response to over 90%.

The quality of responses achieved by this survey was very high and both the parents and the young people seemed able to express their views quite openly. There was no identifiable difference in the replies given in the cases where the Committee Member helped people complete questionnaires, and although she wrote down the answers the language used and views expressed were clearly those of the young person or parent: this group included young people and adults who had mild learning difficulties or literacy problems.

The project used the information gathered in the two ways intended. Reports to the local authority funders drew on anonymous quotes from users, which as one person noted "really brought it to life and showed we work with real people", as well as reporting the detailed findings. The points emphasised by the young people and their parents were slightly different from those normally raised by professionals – for example, both the parents and the children placed considerable stress on people's well-being and relationships within the family ("he is still a pest but more settled in himself" "my Mum doesn't look so worried" "I don't fight my brother as often") and less on changed behaviour. These points have been taken on board by the project in their regular reviews. The project has also changed some aspects of the way parents are initially contacted about referrals to the project, which they now undertake themselves. One point which came through very clearly was the children's and parents' difficulties in communicating with some staff at local schools. The project is now trying to take this on in meetings with the headteachers about how they respond to disruptive and unsettled pupils.

Notes

This survey had a "pilot" stage when they did a "dummy run" of the questionnaires. This is a very important part of preparing for any means of asking questions but especially when using written forms. If you are asking people questions and realise you have missed out something important, or if the question is phrased awkwardly, you can usually put it right after the first few interviews, but it is a lot worse to realise this as you are reading through a 100 or so completed forms. Have a pilot stage if it is at all possible. Perhaps the quickest and most productive way of doing this is what was done here – ask a few people who are in the same situation as your target audience to fill up the form (or ask them the questions if that is what you are planning) and then check with them whether the questions were easy to understand or unclear and if the layout made it easy to complete, etc. This is your last opportunity to check if there are any points you have missed, so your guinea pigs' "other comments" are worth special attention. If you did not have the time or opportunity for a pilot, at least check out your plans with other people who know your users, as the project did in Case Example 11.

For written questionnaires or forms the layout of the pages is almost as important as the wording of the questions. Make sure you have given people enough space to note their answers (but not too much). If possible, use different type faces or capital letters to make the questionnaire easier to understand.

The questionnaires in this case example, which are attached at the end, used a mix of *closed questions*, (yes/no or "tick box") where the person chooses between suggested answers, and *open questions*, where the person can give the answer they choose. Tick-box questions make the questionnaire quicker and easier for the person filling it in. They are also easier to analyse: the section in the last part of the handbook shows how to do this. These questions are good for factual points where you can anticipate what the answers are likely to be or where you can reflect a range of views. The open questions are better where you want more detail or where you want to give the people answering the questions a completely free hand. Again, the section at the end of the handbook shows you how to go about pulling these comments together.

This project secured an exceptionally high response rate which is a remarkable – but very uncommon – achievement. In other circumstances a response rate of around 60% would be a realistic target. However, the reasons for this exceptional response appear to be:

- being able to contact all the target group: no one had moved out of the area and the few families who had moved house were very easily traced;

- the role of the Committee Member securing virtually all the outstanding returns;

- the high level of interest in the service among the users/target respondents; and

- a rare opportunity for the users to comment on some related issues – such as contact with schools – about which they held fairly strong views.

With hindsight, the Steering Group thought they should have realised some people would have difficulties completing a written form and made other arrangements. However the arrangement eventually used was very suitable, both in effectiveness and in avoiding any element of stigma. A similar approach was used intentionally – for similar reasons – in one of the day care centres for older people, which is described in the Age Concern for Scotland booklet.

SMITHSHIRE COMMUNITY YOUTH PROJECT

SURVEY OF YOUNG PEOPLE USING THE PROJECT

Your name:

Address:

Age when you joined the Project:

---

1. Did you come to

please tick one

☐   only one group

☐   more than one group or block

2. What type of group did you come to:

please tick one   *please tick one*

☐   day   ☐   mixed

☐   evening   ☐   single sex

3. How did you feel about coming to the Project?

4. Overall, did you enjoy coming to the group?

☐ a lot   ☐ a bit,   ☐ not often   ☐ not at all
               sometimes

Are there any parts of the group you especially enjoyed?

Are there any bits you really disliked?

5. While you were at the group, was the help you got from project staff
☐ very good   ☐ quite good   ☐ not good   ☐ not good at all

6. Did you feel you got any help from the other members in your group?
☐ lot of help,   ☐ some help   ☐ not much   ☐ no help at all
part of a team   help

7. Did you get any encouragement from your parents and family ?
☐ good support   ☐ some support   ☐ not much   ☐ no help at all
and help   and help   help

8. Did you get any encouragement or help from your teachers?
☐ good support   ☐ some support   ☐ not much   ☐ no help at all
and help   and help   help

9. Have you wanted to keep in touch with the Project staff since you left the group?   **yes / no**

If yes, have you been able to do this?   **yes / no**

10. What did you get from coming to the Project?

11. In what ways do you think being a member of a group helped you?

12. Had you heard of the SYP before you came to the group?   **yes / no**

Do other people in your area know of the Project?   **yes / no**

What do they think of it?

Are there any other comments you would like to make about the Smithshire Youth Project?

THANK YOU FOR YOUR HELP

Please return this form to   Mrs Mary Jones
Smithshire Youth Project
1 High Street, Markettown

SMITHSHIRE COMMUNITY YOUTH PROJECT

SURVEY OF PARENTS OR GUARDIANS OF CHILDREN USING THE PROJECT

Your name:

Address:

Name of child who used Smithshire Youth Project:

Your relationship to child:

---

1. Who suggested to you that your child might attend the Smithshire Youth Project [SYP]?

2. At the time, did you feel the reason for this was explained?

please tick one

☐   properly explained

☐   not properly explained [eg only partly, rushed]

☐   not explained

Please add any comments :

3. How did you feel at that time about your child coming to the Project?

4. What do you think was the purpose of your child coming to the Project?

Do you think this was achieved?

please tick one

☐   was achieved

☐   partly achieved

☐   not achieved

Please add any comments on
-the aspects you thought went well

-the aspects you thought were not so successful

5. What benefits did your family get from the project?

- for the child who came to the Project

-for parents

- for others in family, especially brothers and sisters

6. How did the Project keep in touch with you and your partner?
[eg home visits
phone calls]

Did the SYP staff tell you the things you wanted to know?

Did you feel able to contact them?

7. What do you feel about your involvement in the Project as a parent?

☐   about right

☐   would have liked to be more involved

☐   would have liked to be less involved

8. Had you heard of the SYP before your child became involved?

yes / no

Do other people in your area know of the Project?

What do they think of it?

Are there any other comments you would like to make about the Smithshire Youth Project?

THANK YOU FOR YOUR HELP

Please return this form to   Mrs Mary Jones
Smithshire Youth Project
1 High Street, Markettown

CASE EXAMPLE 10

User feedback: survey by workers

Background and Circumstances

In the situation described in Case Example 9, someone from the project got feedback from some users by asking them the questions on the questionnaire – what is called an "administered survey" rather than a "self-completion survey". In some situations this is the best way to obtain information and is the approach planned from the outset.

The Project

An example of this is a Family Centre which provided a range of services to families living in the local area, which is one of considerable social and economic deprivation. One of these activities was "Building Blocks" – this was similar to a mother and toddler group but focused more strongly on learning-based play with trained volunteers working alongside the parents of pre-nursery children. The aim was to help the children develop language and other skills so they would gain more from nursery school when they enrolled a year or so later. It was also hoped to give some of the parents – for example, young mothers with no close family or friends – more confidence in playing with their children and give them some company and support. In some cases the children's behaviour was more disruptive than their parents could easily cope with, which added to other stresses and further reduced the likelihood of the children settling at nursery and primary school. A home-visiting scheme was linked to the project, involving volunteers and project staff.

Users had the opportunity to express views and ideas through the project's Advisory Group and other channels, but the staff wanted to hear how *all* users viewed the service. They were also keen to discover how far parents thought the scheme's aims had been achieved and identify the impact, if any, on the relevant aspects of the family's life. They set out to get an overview of the scheme's progress, but if it emerged that some families were not benefiting the plan was to follow this up with the family and explore other options.

The main reasons for having someone ask the questions, rather than give people a form to fill in, were:

- the project felt it was important to include as many users as possible, so the aim was for as high a response as possible;

- it was thought that even a fairly simple form would pose problems for some users, whose literacy skills were limited;
- it was doubtful if a written form would adequately cover users' assessments of changes in their child's behaviour or in personal relationships;
- time and care had been spent in building up a relationship with mothers and it was thought that giving them a form to fill in would seem a bit cold and unfriendly, especially as many users were in any case apprehensive about forms which they associated with poll tax collection.

What Was Done

The survey was carried out over a month. Users were kept informed about the plans for the survey and how it would be used. The interviews were done at the users' homes by a volunteer or a staff member who was known to that user but had *not* worked closely with them. Interviewers were able to discuss questions with the user and the wording of all answers recorded by the interviewer was that decided by the user. Users were free to complete the form themselves if they wished, so the layout took account of this. In the event, two mothers wished to discuss the topics with a partner or relative and return the form later.

The project considered this feedback exercise to have been a success. Almost all parents participating in the scheme were included (4 refusals or cancelled visits from 19 parents). Overall, the standard of the returns was high. Workers were able to help users reflect on changes in their child's behaviour and this sometimes became more akin to a case work interview than a traditional research interview. However, there is no reason to believe staff influenced users' views.

The cost of this, however, was a high demand on the time of the staff and volunteers concerned. It was sometimes necessary to set up three or more visits before obtaining a completed questionnaire: although this is common to many research surveys people still found it frustrating, especially when demands from work and other commitments were high. Some interviews were brief (15-20 minutes) but others took considerably longer, especially when the user and interviewer discussed some matters at length before noting a relatively brief response. However, the time taken was generally considered well spent by the project staff.

The completed questionnaires were analysed by the project co-ordinator by counting the number of times each pre-coded ("tick box" type or yes/no) reply was given and identifying key words for answers to open questions.

The findings were fed back to users by displaying a large poster-type list of the main points. These were discussed, along with what ought to be done, at a specially arranged meeting with users a few weeks later: this included looking at changing the times and frequency of the group and aspects of the physical layout. The report was also given to the Advisory Group and to staff in schools and the Social Work Department with whom the project worked. Some points were included in the project's next annual report, which had a wider distribution among policy-makers and senior managers in the local authority.

Generally the survey showed that the parents and their children enjoyed Building Blocks and benefited from it. The replies showed that this scheme was not meeting the needs of a few users. However, this was discussed among the project team, and some ways of meeting the needs of parents who were particularly isolated and experiencing multiple problems were again considered in the project's forward planning. These ideas were discussed with the families concerned in the course of the scheme's on-going contact with them and some people were offered a more intensive one-to-one contact with their child and/or additional support or services for the mother to supplement the Building Blocks scheme.

NORTHSIDE FAMILY RESOURCE CENTRE : BUILDING BLOCKS

SURVEY OF PARENTS

This survey is being done to find out what the users think about Building Blocks. Your replies will help us to improve this and other services.
All information given will be treated in confidence.

Please add extra comments at any point if you wish

How helpful have you found Building Blocks?
tick one box

☐   very good ☐   not helpful
☐   quite helpful ☐   very poor

What do you think are the best aspects?

Are there any things you don't like?

How did you get on with the Building Blocks Leaders?
tick one box

☐   very well ☐   a bit difficult at times
☐   quite well, or OK ☐   very difficult

Do you feel the Building Blocks Leaders involve you in what they do?
tick one box

☐   yes
☐   sometimes, or for some things
☐   not involved

Has your child enjoyed the sessions?

Have you enjoyed the sessions you took part in?

Have you enjoyed the parent - run sessions you took part in?

Can you explain why?

How are you [and your partner] getting on with your child these days?

Does your child ever have difficult behaviour?

Compared to before you began coming to Building Blocks, is this happening
tick one box
☐ more often than before
☐ less often than before
☐ about the same

Is the difficult behaviour
tick one box
☐ better than before
☐ worse than before
☐ about the same

Are you [and your partner] able to cope with the difficult behaviour
tick one box
☐ better than before
☐ worse than before
☐ about the same

Has **your child** benefited from coming to Building Blocks?   **YES / NO**

If Yes, can you say in what ways?

If No, can you think of anything which would have helped?

Have **you** benefited from Building Blocks?   **YES / NO**

If <u>Yes</u>, in what ways?

If <u>No,</u> can you think of anything which would have helped?

How do you feel your child will get on when she/he goes to nursery school?

Would you be interested in coming to workshops where you could learn more about

	YES	NO
play	☐	☐
child development	☐	☐
early education	☐	☐
preparing for nursery school	☐	☐

Are there any other comments you wish to make about Building Blocks?

Are there any comments you wish to make about services at Northside Family Resource Centre?

THANK YOU FOR YOUR HELP

Please return this form to one of the Building Blocks Leaders, or hand it in to the Northside Family Resource Centre.

CASE EXAMPLE 11

User feedback through group discussions

Background and Circumstances

The last two case examples focused on situations where each person's views were sought on an individual basis. However, as the Table on page 84 showed, sometimes it is more appropriate to get feedback from groups of people. Situations where this is especially useful are:

- when time is too short for sending out forms or asking each person individually;

- you are more interested in the range of views than the exact number of people holding such views; or

- you are not certain what the range of ideas and opinions will be, so drawing up a list of questions – particularly the "tick-box" type – is difficult.

The Project

This was a community-based resource providing a wide range of services to children and their parents living in the town and, in particular, in the surrounding estate. Many of the families using the project had complex and long-standing social problems. The project had an open access arrangement where anyone could come along if they thought the project had something to offer. It also accepted formal referrals from the Social Work Department and other formal sources. To avoid any stigma the project aimed to provide services which could potentially attract people from a wide range of social circumstances.

Most of the project's activities were group-based – after-school group for younger children, summer playschemes, boys' and girls' clubs in the early evenings for 8-12 year olds and youth club-type activities for teenagers.

There was a range of groups for parents – usually mothers. These included adult literacy classes, a local residents' group, a group for new parents and the International Women's group, which included the wives of students at a local university and women from Asian families living in the town. A creche was provided for all these groups and mothers and toddlers group met two days each week. There was also an open play/chat facility for everybody (parents and children) on Saturday mornings.

The project wanted to obtain feedback from users on a range of issues:

- their general views of the project;

- comments on particular aspects to help the project plan for possible changes – for example, concerning the premises, expansion to other parts of the town and changes to the referral criteria;

- the value of particular group activities; and

- benefits to users and members of their family.

What was Done

The project staff discussed at a team meeting the kind of things they wanted to learn from the users. It was decided that some of the matters suggested were too personal and should be followed up in other ways. It was agreed to ask everyone about the same matters, even though some points were likely to be of greater concern to some groups of users than to others. From this the coordinator drew up a list which covered the main topics for the parents and other adults. A shorter list was then made for the children and young people. The coordinator sounded out a few volunteers who worked with the groups for their ideas and comments and the two lists were then finalised at the next staff meeting. A copy of the lists is at the end of this case example.

The reasons for using group discussions for this feedback rather than individual questionnaires were:

- timing and resources: the project committee wanted to submit a report to the local authority within a few months and the project could not gather the views of over 100 users individually;

- this was less anxious for the users: many people within the project were very apprehensive about being asked to fill in forms, had limited literacy skills and may have been unwilling to express views of personal experiences which would be connected only with them;

- the project was more concerned at this stage with getting feedback about general issues and options than about the impact for specific individuals. There were other means of getting feedback from individuals who made extensive one-to-one use of the project about changes in their personal situation.

The actual discussions for each group all took place during a fortnight. Each

H

group organiser (a member of staff, volunteer, user or other person) started the discussion off, using the list as the basis, and making sure all the points were covered.

The adults were consulted about the plan to hold this discussion at their meeting the previous week, while the children were asked if they wanted to participate at the start of the relevant session. None of the groups decided not to have the discussion and most people welcomed the chance to express their views and discuss these aspects of the project. Some adult groups used this opportunity for a wide-ranging discussion about the project and their discussion took a whole session. The children's discussions tended to be shorter and more focused. Both the adults and children were mixed in whether one person (the organiser or a member of the group) acted as scribe for a shared, agreed response or whether they also completed individual responses on copies of the list after the discussion. Sometimes the conversation covered personal views and experiences and sometimes references were more impersonal – for example, "people might think/feel that ......" and "people like us would .....".

How the Replies were Analysed

The project coordinator gathered together the schedules and went on to identify key phrases in the same way as for the other feedback surveys described in this handbook. Because a single form does not represent the views of one person, these could simply not be added up to find the number of people holding a particular view. She therefore focused on which groups – either the whole group or individuals within it – had made certain comments: this is shown in detail in the section on how to analyse information in Part 3 at pages 192-3.

This feedback demonstrated that all the groups were valued by their users, but in different ways.

"Its good to learn from other mums – just ordinary folk, not the experts."

"Its good for the kids to have different children to play with."

The general view was that the most interesting responses came from the children, especially, the 5-8 year olds, who were well aware of the project's aim to provide a safe haven and opportunity for children to raise matters of concern:

"We have nowhere else to go and we feel welcome and liked here."

"We get to make things and have someone to talk to if we are angry or not happy."

How the Feedback was Used

The information was used in the report to the project's Committee and to the local authority. Plans to tighten the referral criteria in order to target the resources more efficiently were put aside, as the feedback showed that this would in fact discourage those current and potential users most in need of the service. There had been strong support for a health visitor and a few other professionals who had worked with users through the project. After the report was circulated it was followed up at a meeting between the project staff and professionals from a range of other services to look at ways they could link in successfully to activities at the project.

Notes

This project already had a network of groups so it could link in this feedback exercise very easily. In other circumstances a project would have to organise one or more groups especially for this purpose, which would mean spending more time and effort.

In this case the people already knew each other and knew that others would understand their points of view, even if they did not always share them. There were also experienced, trained volunteers and staff who knew how to handle groups of people – what to do if someone got upset or angry, or if the discussion got out of hand. There are likely to be fewer potential problems if the subject being discussed is not too personal or controversial. However if you were at all uncertain about handling a group it would be a good idea to get advice or bring in someone to help.

USERS' VIEWS OF THE EASTSIDE COMMUNITY PROJECT
Children and young people

Group:

The Project
1. Is the community flat a good idea?

2. What are the best bits of the project?

3. Are there any bits you don't like?

4. Are there any other things you would like it to do?

5. Would it be a good idea to have a community flat in other parts of Eastside?

This Group
1. Do you enjoy coming to this group?

2. What do you think the group is for?

3. What do you get out of coming to the group? [for example, making friends, someone to talk to]

4. Do other people in your family like you coming to the group?

Are there any other things you want to tell us about the Eastside Project?

Thank you for your help

USERS' VIEWS OF THE EASTSIDE COMMUNITY PROJECT [Adults]

Group:

A. The Project

1. Is the community flat a good idea?

2. Is the community flat good for the area?

3. What are the best features of the project?

4. Some other services and people [like Health Visitors] use the project as a base:

   –what services/people are useful?

   –are there any services/people you would like to see at the project?

   –are there any other services/people you would not like to see at the project?

5. What do you think of the premises at 130 Side Street:

   –is it big enough?

   –the layout and facilities?

   –location?

6. Would other parts of Eastside benefit from a local community flat like this one?

B. This Group

1. What do you see the group as being for?

2. Do you enjoy coming to the group?

3. What do you get from coming to the group?

4. Do your children or other members of your family get any benefit from your coming to this group?

5. What do you think other people think about the people who come to this group?

C. Other Parts of the Project

1. Do you like being able to drop in at other times?

2. Have you used the Home Support?
  - did you find it useful?

Are there any other things you wish to tell us about the Project?

Thank you for your help.

CASE EXAMPLE 12

User feedback from on-going contact

Background and Circumstances

Often users of services give feedback through their day-to-day contact – by telling the staff what they think of the service, mentioning ways they have benefited or activities they have been able to do with consequence of the service. All projects listen to this type of feedback, especially in relation to the needs and circumstances of those individual people. The feedback exercises described in the earlier examples in this section have often been prompted by these kinds of comments and were designed to supplement this on-going communication by having an intentional "stop and think" by openly asking people for their ideas and views. This then became the basis of thinking about the progress of the project overall. However sometimes it is not appropriate to raise this with users and so the only feedback from users which the project has is this informal type. It then becomes a question of how to record and use this in an appropriate way.

The Project

This service provided daytime care for older people with dementia. It provided intensive support – usually five afternoons or early evenings each week – and linked in to social work and health care services. There was a small number of users, usually no more than ten at any time. The aim of the project was to support very vulnerable people in the community and thus avoid or delay long-stay hospital care. A second aim was to support carers, and the project placed considerable emphasis on their needs. A support group, at which carers would meet to discuss problems and share ideas and experiences met monthly. The project also had frequent contact with the carers as part of their day-to-day work. Where a user was living with relatives project workers had met the carers every day, for example when picking people up to bring them to the centre or taking them home. There was also frequent contact with those relatives who lived away from the elderly person with dementia. There were frequent 'phone calls to virtually all the other carers and regular home visits to those people who lived relatively nearby.

Inevitably relatives gave a lot of feedback to project workers in the course of these conversations. After a month or two the project staff discussed the need to write this down. This was prompted by two separate issues:

- the need to record information about changes in users' and carers' circumstances, given the advanced state of the illness for this group of people. It was likely that changes could occur in their condition or their circumstances quite quickly. The project had to be able to note changes in the pattern of someone's well-being if they were to respond to this by offering an increased service or making sure the person got access to appropriate health care or other support; and

- they needed to gather information about users' views and experiences to help them improve and develop the service and to give initial feedback to the funders and other agencies with which they worked, as some of the people concerned still had reservations about the need and value of such an intensive service.

However the project workers were reluctant to simply ask people what they thought of the service through a survey or discussions, as was done elsewhere. There were several reasons why they felt such an approach would be wrong at this stage:

- it was still too early – the scheme had only been delivering care for a few months;

- the project had put a lot of effort into building a relationship with the carers and did not want to suggest that they had not been listening to the feedback and ideas people were telling them anyway;

- many of the families had bad experiences of case reviews and similar occasions when they had been asked their views about services and about their relative's needs, as this had led to the service being withdrawn because their relative was too ill or demanding or because the other services were considered not to be meeting their needs.

The project therefore decided to design a sheet to systematically record the feedback that was being given to workers in the course of ordinary conversations. At one of their regular team meetings the project workers – both staff and volunteers – listed out the kinds of things which people were telling them. Although the details of this varied a lot from case to case, there were several main topics which were fairly common. The co-ordinator and secretary then drew up a sheet which had these topics as the main headings. During the next month staff and volunteers noted the feedback which carers had given them when they returned to the office. They only noted a few key words and did not necessarily fill in a sheet after every visit. For the first week or two people tended to note down a great deal of detail but after discussing it they soon settled into a pattern where only the main relevant information was recorded. After about a month, at the next team meeting, the workers considered any changes they wanted to make to the sheet. The main thing that was added at this point was the "action taken" column. In practice, any points of concern were acted on immediately, as staff had done before. However this meant that they were then making separate notes on the person's case file. This change enabled them to minimise the paperwork and was also a double check that important information had been acted upon.

After three months the coordinator went through all the sheets and pulled together the information for each person on a summary form (exactly the same as the other forms) for each person. This covered whether the feedback about the project and the people's circumstances was generally positive or negative, and throughout specific issues which had been raised. She then pulled together the information for all the users and prepared a short report on this. This report was discussed internally among the project staff, who then considered ways in which they could deal with some of the points which carers had been making. The report was also discussed with the project's Management Group. Some of the points were then raised at the carers' support group over the next few meetings, as and when these points came up in conversation. This was raised along the lines of "some carers are mentioning to us that .... is this also how other people feel?" etc.

Points to Note

• This way of noting feedback from users is clearly very closely related to the kind of detailed case notes which many projects providing intensive services are keeping anyway. The main difference here is the way in which the information is used. However this kind of approach can be used on a long-term basis as part of the general recording system of this type of project.

• This approach does have its limitations. Just because users do not raise particular points in the course of their comments to the staff does not mean that they are not concerned about a matter or hold views on it. Users may mention the most urgent matter and not have time or feel this is not the right place to discuss other points. Some care also has to be taken that the workers do not distort what users are saying. Some of the ways in which this can be tackled are discussed in more detail in the next case example.

• It is always better to openly check the points back with the users if at all possible. One way to do this is the method used here, where points were checked back with the carers at their regular meeting. Over time, this project planned to go on to introduce more formal feedback systems. This was done in similar circumstances by another project, this time providing respite care and home-based support for families with a profoundly disabled child. Here the project noted the main types of feedback coming from users over the first few months. However after about a year they did a survey of their users, following up points which some users had raised over the course of the day-to-day feedback.

• As well as gathering feedback from users, the approach developed here has a lot of potential in providing information about the outcomes for users, especially those in circumstances such as the people here, where the situation can change quickly and/or the people involved are themselves not always able to be objective.

CARER FEEDBACK SHEET

User: Date:

Carer: Worker:

ISSUES RAISED   ACTION TAKEN

User's general well-being

Changes in User's Circumstances

Recent behaviour (wandering, violent outbursts)

Carers' general well-being, coping

Change in Carer's circumstances

Views about Project

Users' feedback to carer about project

Other matters

CASE EXAMPLE 13

User feedback: case work interview

Background and Circumstances

Most of the projects described in these case examples are providing care to users over many months or years. They know who their users are and often have an on-going relationship with them. Some projects, however, take the form of briefer contacts such as drop-in information and advice centres and telephone advice lines. These can be used on a one-off basis or, in some instances, as a series of contacts ranging over months or even years. Here, the user chooses to come to the service for a specific purpose and usually has a large degree of control over the level and detail of information given. Sometimes the user's personal circumstances are not relevant – for example, in the case of queries about consumer goods to a Citizens' Advice Bureau. In other situations the person may wish anonymity – for example, counselling and advice lines offering support and information to people with HIV/AIDS, parents feeling pressured and at risk of hitting their children, carers of elderly relatives, or people who have been abused or hurt in some way.

Despite these limits, however, the counsellors or advisers often feel that they know from their communication with users what the other person's views of the service are, especially when the counsellor has several years' training and experience.

Assessing how well services such as these are meeting user needs poses many challenges. Conventional approaches to obtaining user feedback are often not available. It would not be possible, for example, to send someone a questionnaire when you do not know their name or where they live. Similarly it may not be appropriate to raise these matters directly at the end of the contact.

Most evaluations which have been undertaken of services of this type have focused on the service as a whole – for example, charting trends in the overall numbers of users – on the assumption that if the service is good users will return and give friends a positive report, while word will also get around about a poor service. Another established method is an assessment of the process – for example, quality of the volunteers' training, whether the advice given follows agreed standards and guidelines: this has often involved another person such as a supervisor listening in to a sample of calls or visits. Approaches such as these have many strengths and are an important part of any complete assessment, but take little account of experiences and views expressed directly or indirectly by users.

The Project

A telephone advice and counselling service for families was to have a wide scale review of the service. It already had information on some aspects which suggested how well they were doing, but wanted to have more feedback from users.

Information was already available on the number and length of calls and a brief classification of the content of the request or problem. If a person gave details such as name, age and location this was noted, but not routinely asked. Information relevant to the case – for example the ages of children, the condition of the vulnerable person being cared for – was noted, especially for longer counselling calls and repeat/follow-on calls. If a caller wanted to discuss an issue further they would be offered a day and time when that counsellor was available and the project often made the return call. One of the issues the project particularly wanted to look at was the type and quality of service provided in these follow-up calls.

The project already had a system of supervision, where the work of individual volunteers was discussed between them and an experienced volunteer or the co-ordinator, and monthly team meetings which sometimes included practice issues.

What Was Done

The Co-ordinator and Manager drew up a list of points of information which they thought were needed about the service, focusing on the quality of the counsellor's input and outcomes for the user. The intention was, as far as possible, to look for feedback from the caller within the conversation to establish these points. This was discussed with volunteers at a team meeting and refined further, and a schedule was then drawn up by the co-ordinator: this is attached at the end of this example. The schedule was to be completed by the counsellor during, or immediately after, each call received over a two week period.

The team discussed in considerable detail how they would tackle this exercise. At the next monthly meeting, the co-ordinator and a volunteer acted out a couple of recent calls and the rest of the team completed schedules on this. Once the feedback exercise was up and running the co-ordinator also took a small sample of completed schedules and went over the way these had been recorded, rather than the content of the call, with the counsellor. Largely as a result of these steps, the team had a fairly high level of consistency and objectivity in the way the information was recorded.

The team were anxious that any positive benefits claimed would be attributed to their "putting a rosy glow on it" and made a conscious decision that unless a clear reason was evident for a positive outcome they would not record anything. As such, it is likely that the skills and achievements of this project were under-estimated in this exercise.

At the end of the two week period the co-ordinator analysed the information obtained. The project did not have access to a computer so this was all done manually. About half the schedule was pre-coded and for most of the other questions a key-word system was used, based largely on the earlier discussions within the team. At several points (for example, question 5b, 14) the schedule asked for comments on responses: this was used to verify the counsellor's response and could mostly be excluded from the analysis. Using the case references, the co-ordinator was able to link the information on the schedule to that already available in the routine record book, so the analysis and report were able to cover all relevant information without the counsellors having to note this twice.

The results of this study showed that there were some marked differences between the circumstances of first and repeat calls, in the way counsellors responded to these, and the outcomes for the users. It also showed that counsellors responded in different ways to different types of requests and behaviour/feedback by the caller.

The findings from this user feedback exercise were used in the review report and for planning within the project. Some of the points from this review were incorporated into training for existing and new counsellors. The project also drew on the information when considering the type of services they provided, especially to people with more complex problems looking for a substantial counselling input.

Other Situations

Another situation where this casework approach was taken to obtaining feedback from users was when residents were leaving a service for young homeless people. Users were with the project for periods ranging from a few days to several months, during which the project sought to help the young person find and successfully retain accommodation. Apart from the initial referral/assessment interview most contact between the users and project staff was through informal day-to-day conversations. Given the intensity of the relationship, circumstances of the users and ethics of the project it was considered inappropriate to give people written questionnaires.

However, in virtually every case the person had a relatively informal interview/meeting with a member of staff to deal with matters such as exchanging keys or documents, leaving a forwarding address and reminding the user of the scope for further contact. Matters which were covered in each case included confirmation of what services the person would be using, whether any problems were expected and how the person's views of the project had changed. The staff members specifically invited the users to give their assessment, but usually in a conversational way.

After the person had left the staff member noted the main points on a short form, which is attached at end of the example. This focused on services which the person would be using over the next few weeks or months and the main points of feedback raised during the conversation.

Notes

As with several of the other case studies in this guide, the longer, more detailed recording schedule could be used if the feedback was to be gathered for only a few weeks, or if the project worked with only a small number of cases. If there was a larger volume of cases and/or this was to be done regularly – as in the second example – a shorter version would be better.

If a project began gathering feedback from users in this way, ie. based on casework interviews, it would be a good idea to reconsider the *method* of gathering feedback every so often. Clearly it is better if people have the opportunity to state their own views directly whenever possible and it may be possible to change to a short feedback questionnaire or interview given at the end of the interview or discussion.

This approach is more prone than most to claims that the findings are influenced or filtered by the people providing the service. Steps that appear to make this approach as useful and as objective as possible include:

- having a high level of agreement among staff about what information is relevant, how they would describe certain statements or behaviour, etc; and
- someone checking and/or discussing a sample of forms to ensure standards are maintained in how information is recorded.

Midtown Helpline : Feedback from Callers

Note to Counsellors
Fill in a form for each call you take between 1/2/91 and 15/2/91.
Also fill in the Record Book in the usual way.

Case No: _____

1. Is this a repeat call   ☐

      first call   ☐

2. How did the interview begin?

☐ referred by another service
☐ questioning type of service
☐ reluctant caller
☐ pouring out problem

3. What do you think the caller's expectations were?

☐ information
☐ advice
☐ someone to talk to

Other comments:

4. How would you describe the caller's demeanour at the start of the call?

5a. Immediate / presenting problems:

5b. If this is a repeat call, is the nature of the call

☐ same as before?
☐ different?

Comments:

6. Were there other agencies involved at this stage?   YES / NO

If yes, please list:

7. What did you as a counsellor do at this stage?

tick as many as apply   Notes:
☐ listened actively
☐ explored problem
☐ clarified problem
☐ helped caller to understand problem
☐ helped caller to work out a plan of action
☐ suggested alternative support systems
☐ gave advice
☐ gave information
☐ referred to another agency
other:

8. What skills and knowledge did you use?

9. Who did most of the talking?

10. Did you feel that you were given enough information to move the caller on to the next stage?

Did you feel that the caller was holding informaton back?

Please comment:

11. Other problems revealed or identified?

12. To what extent was the caller able to express his/her feelings?

13. What kind of relationship was established?

Please comment:

14. Do you think the caller may have felt threatened?

Comments:

15. How did the caller benefit from your intervention?

tick as many as apply   Notes:
☐ given space to talk
☐ referred on appropriately
☐ decided on a plan of action
☐ has a greater understanding of his/her
      problem
☐ feels supported, sustained
☐ less stressed, worried, anxious etc.
☐ prevented situation getting worse
☐ prevented statutory involvement
☐ maintained the status quo
☐ averted a crisis situation
other:

16. How do you feel other agencies may have benefitted from your intervention?

☐ appropriate referral made
☐ time was not wasted
☐ caller now has clear needs or expectations to present
☐ reinforced the role and remit of agency

other:

Notes:

17. In what ways do you feel that other members of the caller's family may have benefited from your intervention?

18. What was agreed with the caller?

19. What goals were set?

20. Which agencies were used for onward referral?

21. Do you expect the caller to ring back?

☐ yes : **why?**

☐ no : **why not?**

22. Duration of call?   ___hour   _____ mins

Did you make a return call?   YES / NO

If yes, reason:

What do you think influenced the length of the call?

23. Can you make a comparison between the caller's demeanour at the beginning and at the end of the call?

Describe in detail:

24. How do you as a counsellor feel at the end of the call?

25. Reflecting on the caller's expectations and needs at the beginning of the call - were these met?

Please comment in detail

CLOSING INTERVIEW : USER FEEDBACK

Name: _____   Case ref: _____ / _____

Services to be used: Any difficulties expected by user?:

	Yes	No
1.	☐	☐
2.	☐	☐
3.	☐	☐
4.	☐	☐

Type of accommodation person is going to: *[tick one]*

public rented flat or house	☐	family	☐
private rented flat or house	☐	friend	☐
Bed and Breakfast	☐	other :	

Notes, Comments about housing or support arrangements:

User's general view of project

Views and feelings expressed in interview
about situation / leaving project:

about project generally or service received:

Specific comments:
aspects of project which were helpful:

which were not helpful:

where more input was needed:

on relationship with staff:

with other users:

5

Feedback from agencies

The last section looked at ways of getting feedback from the people who use our services. It is also important for a project to get feedback from workers in other agencies. There are two reasons for this.

1. They can give another view of what happens to the users. It was noted in the section on outcomes how other service providers, such as the GP of a frail older person using a day care centre, can be in a good position to know how that person is doing and what changes have happened over the last year or so. They may also know something of the wider benefits or outcomes – for example what is happening to other members of the family – and see this differently from the people themselves.

2. Workers in other settings can themselves benefit from your project. Sometimes the projects are specifically designed to help staff elsewhere, for example by providing specialised resource or additional skills to complement existing services. Staff may develop new skills or benefit from expert advice. Another benefit might be taking pressure off services where there is high demand, freeing places for other users. Some people also find that being able to share responsibility for a group of users or having someone knowledgeable to talk to outside their own organisation eases some of the stress which many people experience when working with especially vulnerable users or in particularly difficult situations.

Sometimes it is important to get this on a case-by-case basis, for example as the project did in Case Example 7 in the Outcome section. Another example of this is given here in Case Example 14, which takes this idea a stage further and combines feedback from the project to staff in the local Social Work Department team with feedback to the project from the social workers.

Many projects which have regular feedback, perhaps through informal channels, from the other staff with whom they work find it useful to have an overview from time to time. The reasons for this are similar to those prompting projects to ask their users for feedback – to check out that the messages being picked up on a day-to-day basis have been properly understood and that the views of those people who do not say much are included. Case Example 15 describes this type of situation.

Both the examples here rely on written forms, rather than all the other means of getting people's views which were described for the personal users, such as group discussion and interviews. Written questionnaires are the most suitable approach given the circumstances of the people we are approaching here – typically they are very busy seeing their clients, having meetings and the like, and are comfortable with written communication. The advantages of using questionnaires are that they can fill in a form at a time convenient to them, if necessary can take time to update or check their recollection of the cases from their files and can reflect on their views of your project and its benefits to them and their service. The disadvantage is that often your survey will just be one of many documents coming to someone's desk and even if they think it is important it may not be the most urgent matter for them to tackle.

As with personal users, getting the right layout and keeping the questionnaire as "user-friendly" as possible is important. It is also important to think about how you will encourage people to return their forms – Case Example 15 describes some interesting ideas on this.

CASE EXAMPLE 14

Survey of professionals or agencies

Background

As projects carry out their day-to-day work staff usually have frequent contact with a range of people in other agencies – especially those who most often refer clients to the project or to whom the project in turn directs users for other or further services. Staff may also see other professionals regularly at meetings such as the local development forum for a particular client group. In these circumstances, project staff will receive and give feedback on services – for example, learning where services integrate smoothly or have caused problems for particular clients.

But the project staff will not know everyone in other agencies who have an interest or view about the service. Projects are likely to have fewer contacts with other professionals who are also important to the service. These would include managers and other senior staff and people based in teams or areas where there are fewer clients shared with the project. Even in the offices with which a project has regular contact the staff may be frequently changing and newer people will know less about the project and/or have different experiences and views of the way it functions and the service it gives to users.

The views and experiences of all these people are important:

- circumstances can change and previous assessments may be less relevant – for example, the impact of any new referral arrangements for another service or the way the project interacts with statutory services;
- potential clients may come into contact with generalist or administrative staff first before ever reaching specialists with whom the project has most contact;
- senior staff may have responsibility for recommending further financial support or in setting policies about when to refer clients on to projects.

The Project

This project provided specialist residential-based services to vulnerable young adults and was aimed at finding them a stable long-term home within the community and ensuring that they had the necessary practical and social skills to live independently. It had been operating for just over two years. Potential demand for the project was very high and it had tightly drawn criteria. The project had to turn away two or three applicants for every person accepted, either because the person was outwith the criteria or because there were no places available.

At the outset, the project had put considerable effort into explaining its role and remit – which was unique for that location – to all the professionals with whom young people in the target group might come into contact. Since the project had opened, a working pattern had emerged of virtually daily contact with a few specialist teams or people with special responsibilities in other agencies which referred clients or provided the follow on accommodation and/or on-going practical support. Even though the project was often full, project staff were becoming aware that some potential users were slipping through the net and that other people were being referred inappropriately. They also knew that some of the Social Work Department and other agency teams had very high turnover rates and some professionals' knowledge of the project and its aims was limited or inaccurate.

This project had secure funding for several years but was soon to have a mid-way review. The project team had a strong commitment to constantly improving the service: they had established a range of methods to gather feedback from users and identify the outcome of services for users in the short and longer-term. The project was also willing to consider and try out adjustments to the way it operated if these were feasible and could lead to a better service for users. The team hoped to use the review to establish the need to widen their focus – possibly with additional resources – to provide on-going support for their former users in the six months or so after they left the project and were living independently. They knew that the views of staff in the relevant statutory agencies would be an important factor in identifying the need for any revision or expansion of the project's remit.

What Was Done

The project decided to conduct a survey of all staff in agencies with whom they worked or who might be expected to have an active interest in services or/and the well-being of the target client group. The details of this were left to the Project Leader and Depute after the general scope had been discussed at a regular project meeting: the project team and users were kept informed of plans, progress and the outcome through the regular channels and had an opportunity to feed in ideas and topics to be covered by the survey.

A list of over 40 people or organisations to be covered was drawn up: this represented a very wide range, including people who had contact with the project every day, those who had very infrequent contact, people who used the project's full range of services and those who were concerned with only one specific aspect. It was decided to prepare a general questionnaire which would address, as far as possible, all these interests, rather than try to address particular questions to respondents in particular circumstances. This questionnaire is attached to the case example along with the covering letter from the Project Leader which accompanied the forms.

The level of response to the questionnaire varied: some respondents replied very quickly while others needed a lot of prompting ("a good mix of bribes and threats"). Understandably, the project staff felt able to cajole practitioners with whom they had a good working relationship to a greater extent than they could with very senior staff. The quality of the responses was generally good, however: a few people sent incomplete replies but most were full and sometimes very thoughtful responses.

A short thank you note was sent to all those who replied, along with a leaflet about the project and/or copy of the first year's annual report to anyone who asked for more information or to the small minority whose replies showed that they had limited knowledge of the project.

The replies were analysed on a database on the project's computer, based on pre-coded answers (the tick-box type of question) or a key word system for the more open parts. A paper was prepared setting out the general replies and, where appropriate, breaking this down according to whether the person used the project a lot or infrequently and the type of agency.

The report was sent to the project liaison committee which included senior representatives of the main statutory agencies. The findings were discussed very fully at the project's staff meeting and the users' meetings. The report was also used in the review meeting with funders.

The survey confirmed the need for extra support for users after they left the project as agencies and staff which had responsibility for this were clearly struggling to provide this preventative/supportive role against competing demands. The general view from the survey was that, given the fairly low level of provision for this client group, any development or expansion of existing services would be helpful. Respondents also identified other issues: some of these were taken up by the project immediately – for example, improving feedback to the initial referrer – while others formed the basis of long-term planning between the project and other agencies working with this client group.

Issues, Other Approaches

1. Many projects have a more straightforward task when getting feedback from professional staff than the project in this Case Example faced. The main factor appears to be whether or not the people being surveyed use the project in the same way – for example, all make referrals – or in a variety of different ways – for example in this situation where the survey covered referrers, senior staff, other people giving a complementary service, etc. In the simpler circumstances it will often be possible to have more precise questions. It will also usually be easier to analyse and describe the answers – for example in a report – since everybody will be talking about the same thing and the number of questionnaires/replies will probably be smaller.

Whether they are all in the same profession – for example all social workers – or a mix – such as social workers, teachers and health visitors – is less important in designing a survey than whether you want to ask them all the same questions. However, you might want to draw attention in your report to any differences in answers given by groups of people (although never to any identifiable individuals as this would break confidentiality).

2. However, the problem of different people – for example, in different agencies – having very different types of contact with a project is quite common. Another project was faced with the situation of a limited number of main groups of professionals (5) but very marked diversity in how these people used the project and even in the type of users whom each group of professionals referred. In these circumstances, the project decided to target a survey on each specific group of respondents – in effect, running 5 mini-surveys at the same time. To do this, they draw up a list of the main issues which they wanted to check with each of the groups of referrers. They then compared lists, taking account of good ideas in one list and adding these to the others and making sure that any common issues were covered in each list, although the individual question might need to be phrased slightly differently. They then devised a front page which covered points like the name of the person filling in the form and the level of contact which that person had had with the project over the past year – for example, number of cases referred, contact with staff on other matters etc.

The project co-ordinator and secretary then had the job of typing and photocopying the finished questionnaires and making sure that the right versions were sent to the appropriate people. When the responses were returned, the replies were all analysed manually: in this case, the project had no option as they had no computer. The report consisted of a page or so summarising the responses of social workers, teachers etc, then a longer section pulling together common issues raised by all the different types of people.

The advantage of this approach was that the questionnaires were more directly applicable to the people who received them, while the project did not have to worry about sorting out the "not applicable" answers to individual questions. In this it was like the straightforward surveys described at 1. above. The disadvantage was that it resulted in more administrative work for the project. In this instance this was not a problem as there was no particular time pressure on the project to complete this survey and other parts of their evaluation work. However, in other circumstances, it could pose major difficulties for projects.

3. The project in the main case example and the one whose experience is described at 2 above both had difficulties getting in replies from the professionals within a reasonable timescale. As was noted in the case example, one approach to this was for project staff to "remind" staff when they saw them, even to the extent of threatening to stay by someone's desk until the form was completed or offering to take someone out to lunch when the reply was done – both tactics which might work well if the project worker already knows the other person well! Another approach which also produced good results was to ask those representatives of the statutory agencies who sat on the project's advisory or management committee to put a notice round the office, encouraging people to fill in the forms and send them back. In similar situations individual people or agencies undertook to do the chasing of colleagues rather than leave this for the project.

In all cases, it was made clear that the project staff or the agency staff were not trying to influence what the professional colleagues said in the questionnaires – the aim was simply to get a reply within a reasonable time. However, all these projects realised that completing questionnaires for voluntary organisations is not the highest priority of staff in busy offices who are faced with many demands on their time, and that pressing people too hard may actually damage the relationships between the project and colleagues in other agencies.

4. All the situations described in the Case Example and these notes have been where a project is seeking the views of colleagues in other agencies as a one-off or for the first time in several years. Sometimes projects will have to obtain written feedback more regularly – perhaps every year. In these circumstances it would not be appropriate to use such an in-depth list of questions – people's views are unlikely to change substantially in a year and they are likely to be less patient with repeated forms. Here, you might want to do a thorough survey in the first year and then follow-up with a shorter list – perhaps one or two pages – covering the main points and focusing on any changes in the past year.

Covering letter from Project

Dear

The Independence Project is currently looking at ways of improving its professional practice and service delivery.

Part of this evaluation process consists of obtaining feedback from agencies, both locally and nationally, who may come into contact with the Project.

It would be of great benefit to us if you could reply to as many questions as possible in the enclosed questionnaire. Not all questions will be of relevance to all organisations.

It would be helpful if returns could reach us by [date]. A reply paid envelope is attached.

We hope that as a consequence we will be able to provide a better service to agencies and ultimately to our clients.

Thank you very much for your co-operation.

Yours sincerely

PROJECT LEADER

INDEPENDENCE PROJECT
CONSUMER QUESTIONNAIRE

Name of person filling in form:

Authority/Agency for whom you work:

Job Title/Position:

Contact Address & Telephone Number:

USE OF PROJECT

Do you mainly use the Independence Project to:-

Please tick one box

☐ make a referral

☐ seek information – specific and practical

☐ seek information – general and advice

☐ other – please explain

☐ do not use the project

If you use the project, how often do you have contact with us?

Please tick one box

☐ rarely, ie less than once a month

☐ infrequently, ie roughly once a month

☐ frequently, ie more than once a month

☐ extensively, ie once a week or more

REMIT OF THE PROJECT

What do you understand the admission criteria of the Independence Project to be?

Are there any additional groups of young people you feel

(a)   this project should accommodate?

(b)   might benefit from this type of facility?

What do you understand are the types of service that the Independence Project offers?

Are there any additional types of care you feel we could usefully provide?

BENEFITS OF THE PROJECT: YOUNG PEOPLE

What type of benefits do you think the young people derive from the Project?

What factors are important to you in assessing the benefits the young people derive from the Project?

BENEFITS FROM THE PROJECT – AGENCIES

What type of benefits do **you** gain from the Project?

What type of benefits does **your organisation gain** from the Project?

GENERAL ASSESSMENT OF THE PROJECT

Are there any features of the Project which you feel are particularly successful?

Are there any features of the Project which you feel could be improved?

Is the information you receive from the Project helpful?

In the longer-term, what developments would you like to see taking place in services for young people

        (a)   by the Independence Project?

        (b)   in general?

Are there any other comments you wish to make about the Independence Project?

THANK YOU FOR YOUR HELP

Please return this form to: Independence Project

                                      1 Main Street Lane

                                      Main Street

                                      ANYTOWN

CASE EXAMPLE 15

Two-way feedback

Background and Circumstances

Many social care projects work closely with other professionals who refer cases to the project when they think that person or family will benefit from the type of input the voluntary project can provide. Sometimes this is just because they hope the person will enjoy the project and it is largely up to the user whether they come along. In other cases, however, the referral to the project is an alternative to something else which the people involved would prefer to avoid. An example of this is a community-based respite care project as an alternative to an elderly or disabled person going into hospital. In this type of situation the person making the referral – such as a doctor or social worker – needs to know if things are working out as hoped or if some other arrangement is needed for this person and family.

Most projects which need to keep the referrers and other professionals informed about each user have arrangements for this. These could be through mechanisms such as formal reviews of case conferences, by frequent informal contacts or through correspondence. However some projects have a mix of referred cases and people reaching them by less formal routes. These may be less likely to have a system for feedback to other agencies which requires making distinctions between users within the project. Instead they may rely on remembering to tell the referrers about progress on cases of particular concern, or relying on the other person asking for an update and telling the project their assessment.

With the introduction of the new community care arrangements – which place more emphasis on regular assessment and review of "care packages" to check they are still meeting users' needs – many projects may well find themselves having to begin more structured feedback arrangements. This will especially apply to voluntary organisations providing services for people who are older, disabled or ill.

The Project

One project facing this situation was a family centre which offered a wide range of services to children and parents. These included after school games, mother and toddler groups, welfare benefits advice, parent craft classes, support groups for parents and one-to-one counselling for children or adults needing extra help. The users included people who had seen the centre when passing, or been told of it by another parent or by people such as teachers, health visitors and social workers, and those who had been referred to the project – usually by a social worker – for a specific reason.

This project had good relations with staff in the local social work team and they often worked closely together, especially when helping a family to get through a particularly difficult period. However the co-ordinator was aware that they were less good at feeding back to the social worker how the family got on over the next few months. She was also concerned that the projects were not checking out the social workers' assessments of what had happened to the families and getting an update for the project on any other developments that had occurred. This had recently become more apparent as the social work team had a high turnover of staff and quite often a different person was dealing with the case six months or a year after the original referral to the project. She also needed feedback from the social workers to help demonstrate that the project was complementing the team's input and not duplicating it or working completely independently.

What Was Done

The co-ordinator discussed her concerns at a project team meeting and with the Team Leader at the Social Work Office. Everyone agreed that something was needed, but that it had to be something simple and not too detailed.

The coordinator drew up a simple A4 sheet, covering:

- a summary of the circumstances of that person and the original reason for referral;
- a note of what services the project had given;
- the project's assessment of what had happened; and
- space for the social worker to give her assessment and comment on the benefits to the user and to the social work department.

About six months after the case was referred the project filled in the top part of the form and sent it on to the social worker who had referred the case. The administrator at the social work team made sure that if that person had moved on the form went to the person dealing with the case now or to the Team Leader. The social worker was to complete the bottom part of the form, take a copy for their files and send it back to the project.

After this arrangement had settled down the co-ordinator discussed how it was going within the project and also with the Team Leader. The project then decided to extend the arrangement to get feedback from other professionals such as Head Teachers at the local nursery and primary schools.

The project used the information for internal management, in particular to make sure they were giving a good quality of service to individual families. They also discussed cases where feedback showed things had not gone smoothly, looking back to consider if they could have done things better.

The information on all these cases was also pulled together and used in the project's next annual report to the funders, which were a different part of the Social Work Department and other statutory agencies.

Points to Note

The actual timing of the feedback in this case was flexible. This was partly to take account of the circumstances of individual cases – sometimes it was more appropriate to get this feedback earlier or later than six months. The project also had an arrangement where they reviewed cases when the groups were winding up at the summer and Christmas holidays, and this was the point when they usually identified cases which needed to be checked out with the referrers. This suited this particular project and the people they worked with and had the advantage of involving no additional work such as a specific review for the purposes of getting feedback. If there was no convenient point like this to latch into a project would need to think about how best to handle this matter of timing.

The project needed a system to make sure that the social worker returned the forms to them. The arrangement eventually used was for the project secretary to send out the forms and mark in the office diary for a month further on. At that point someone phoned up and reminded people which forms had still to come back. This was one of the refinements introduced over the first few months: because the social workers were only occasionally receiving the forms and usually had to check the information they found they tended to put the forms to one side. However the Social Work Team considered that this was important and were happy to be reminded. Similarly, the system was improved by the administrator in the social work office taking responsibility for making sure that the forms reached the right people when they first arrived. As with the original idea and planning, these were things which the co-ordinator discussed and developed with the Team Leader.

The idea of trying an arrangement with one group of people who are keen to help before going on to extend it to others is a good one. It lets you sort out any teething problems with co-operative "guinea pigs" who can give you ideas on how to make it better. When you then involve more people there should be fewer – hopefully no – changes needed, which makes life easier for both you and the people who are providing you with feedback.

FAMILY CENTRE FEEDBACK SHEET   DATE:

Name of Person/Family:

Address:

Date Referred:

Main reason/s:

Input by project for person:

Other inputs for family

Project's assessment of progress so far:

Worker's Initials:

Social Worker's assessment on progress

Notes/Comments on input of Family Centre:

Social Worker's Initials: Date:

Please return this form to the project

6
Organisation of Services

WHY THIS IS NEEDED

*T*he previous sections have looked at aspects of the way users experience the project and its activities – how they use it, what they think of it, the outcomes of their contact with the project. The other side of this is how the people providing these services experienced the project. There are issues of efficiency and effectiveness for the volunteers, staff and managers in the same way as for the users. The monitoring and evaluation of the way services are organised is also part of good planning and management.

Aspects of this include:

- the range of activities done by volunteers and staff,
- how they spend their time,
- whether they have the right skills and experience for this and whether their skills are being well-used,
- how staff and volunteers are recruited and their characteristics (gender, age, ethnicity and other circumstances).
- turnover, especially amongst volunteers
- the role and responsibilities of the Committee and other people such as line managers and advisory groups
- how these groups go about their tasks and whether all the management areas are adequately tackled
- the training needs of the various people
- financial monitoring and planning.

The projects which helped with the preparation for this handbook tackled some of these matters. The three case examples in this section are concerned with volunteers' views on the project and the training they received (Case Example 16) and the range of activities which volunteers and staff carry out (Case Examples 17 and 18). In the course of doing this, however, some other aspects of how the service was organised inevitably cropped up. Other researchers and consultants have identified ways of tackling some of the other issues listed and useful publications and contacts are given in Part 3 of the handbook.

As with other types of monitoring and evaluation tasks described in this handbook, examining and assessing how a service is organised brings its own challenges and technical problems.

•   The first thing to note is that this is often more stressful for the people concerned, at least where it is first introduced, than the other types of monitoring which have been discussed. Perhaps inevitably, people can be anxious that this is being done to assess how well they are doing their job, or to make some other sort of judgement on them as individuals. Managers and other people introducing this type of monitoring need to be very clear when explaining what they are asking people to record and why. As with other types of monitoring and evaluation work, involving people in planning, taking account of what will be relevant to the volunteers and staff when carrying out their work and feeding back information to them are likely to lead to more accurate and useful information – and fewer frayed nerves.

•   Linked to this, it has to be remembered that the volunteers and staff can be expected to have their own list of questions and issues about how the service is organised. For example, in one of the projects mentioned in Case Example 18 it was the staff who initiated this monitoring to back up their case for an increased travel budget.

•   As with the ways of recording how users had contact with the service (in Section 2 on the scale and pattern of use) thought has to be given to whether you want a detailed or more basic picture and whether this is to be a "snapshot" survey of what happens over a particular few weeks or is to be an on-going system. As a general rule, snapshots can be quite detailed if needed, but on-going monitoring needs to be simple and involve minimal extra effort and inconvenience if it is to be sustained over the longer-term.

CASE EXAMPLE 16

Survey of volunteers

Background and Reasons

Many voluntary organisations work with volunteers in a wide range of situations, including direct contact with the service users. In some settings they are the people who have closest contact with the users. Volunteers also can bring additional skills and ideas to projects which complement and extend the input which paid staff can provide. Projects may draw on volunteers' assessments when considering the benefits of the project for individual service users – for example, in the reviews of outcomes outlined in this Handbook. However the volunteers may be asked for their views on the service overall less frequently.

Volunteers are a valuable asset for many projects, with effort and resources spent on their recruitment, training and management. For some projects, this represents the major part of the co-ordinator's and managers' tasks and low recruitment and/or high levels of turnover can pose significant problems. The benefits which volunteers gain from their time with the project are important – for the people themselves and in encouraging them to stay with the project. For these reasons feedback from volunteers on their training, whether they feel they have the right management support and what they gain from the project are an integral part of projects' assessment and planning.

The Project

This project had been working with volunteers for several years. It provided counselling, support and practical activities for teenagers who were having difficulties coping at school or at home. Full-time professional staff provided the main part of the service but one or two volunteers also worked with each group of teenagers – attending the after school sessions and any weekends or days away.

This project was undertaking a thorough review of its services, including feedback from the young people, their parents, social workers, teachers and other people involved with the project. The feedback from the volunteers was intended to contribute to this overall review and to help the project managers assess their present arrangements for training paid and volunteer workers.

What Was Done

The overall evaluation was discussed at project meetings. Volunteers were aware of the purpose of the survey and suggested topics and questions for this and the other questionnaires. The forms could have been answered anonymously, but this group of people decided to identify the responses. The forms were posted out to volunteers' homes with pre-paid envelopes: all the respondents returned them within a week or so of the agreed date. The replies were then collated by the co-ordinator and manager.

Specific feedback of points raised was made to a regular volunteers' meeting, at which it was agreed to revise some aspects of training and on-going support. The results were merged with all the other sources of information on relevant points in the overall report given to funders and other interested people.

Notes

The volunteers in this case were a small, fairly confident group of people who had a high level of openness and trust with each other and with other project staff and mangers. In other situations it may be more appropriate for questionnaires to be anonymous and avoid questions which would identify the person or group they worked with.

This project had not experienced any difficulties with volunteer recruitment, so the survey did not cover this. Other projects probably would at least want to ask a question such as:

How did you come to hear of the [project]?

☐ personal contact   ☐ Volunteer Bureau

☐ item in newspaper   ☐ other

The questions in this example are centred on the groups of young people, but could easily be adapted to situations such as leisure activities or teaching people a sport or other skill. Where the service is more general and the volunteers have contact with all service users – for example, day care for mentally frail older people – or with only one person – for example, a Befriending scheme – it might be more helpful to phrase questions about the project:

6. Did the way in which the project was organised ....

COMMUNITY YOUTH PROJECT

SURVEY OF VOLUNTEERS

Your name:

Address:

_____

1. How long have you been a volunteer with the project?

2. How many groups have you worked with during the past year, ie between August 1989 and June 1990?

Please fill in a pink sheet for <u>each</u> group
Add any comments after any question if you wish

Then please fill in the white section at the back

pink

Name of Group/Course: _____

3. When you were asked to co-work the group, how well did the project plan the work with you?

☐ well planned ☐ mixed ☐ badly planned

comments:

4. While the group was in progress, were you given enough support and advice?

☐ well supported ☐ mixed ☐ not enough support

comments:

5. Were you happy about the way in which your role was understood?

- by you   yes / no

- by the young people   yes / no

- by the staff   yes / no

comments:

6. Did the way in which the group was organised make you feel confident about your role?

☐ confident ☐ mixed ☐ uncertain

comments:

pink

7. How was the closing of the group handled by the project?

☐   sensitively   ☐   mixed   ☐   poorly handled

comments:

<u>If you were on a residential week-end,</u>

8. Did you feel that the residential component was well organised?

☐   well organised   ☐   mixed   ☐   badly organised

comments:

9. Did you enjoy the time?

☐ enjoyed very much   ☐   mixed   ☐   did not enjoy at all

10. Did the young people enjoy the time?

☐   enjoyed very much   ☐   mixed   ☐   did not enjoy at all

Are there any other comments you wish to make about the residential element?

white

11. Looking back, how useful was the training organised by the project?

☐ very useful   ☐ partly useful   ☐ slightly useful   ☐ not useful

comments:

12. How useful was the training provided by other people?

☐ very useful   ☐ partly useful   ☐ slightly useful   ☐ not useful

comments:

13. Are there any topics which should have been included in the training but were not?

14. What benefits have you gained from your work with the project as a volunteer?

15. What benefits do you feel the <u>project</u> has gained from you and the other volunteers?

16. What benefits do you think the young people and their families have gained from the project?

-the young people

- their families

15. In what ways would you like to see the project develop over the next few years?

Are there any other comments you would like to make about the Project?

THANK YOU FOR YOUR HELP

Please return this form to:
[name of co-ordinator
Project's address]

CASE EXAMPLE 17

Monitoring workers' activities: range of activities

Background and Circumstances

Most projects have a group of people – the co-ordinator, care workers, a secretary or administrator – doing different tasks which complement each other. There are job descriptions for the various functions and everyone is fairly clear about what they, and everyone else, are doing. There are some situations where things are less clear-cut. One reason is when people are doing similar things. This happens when there are, for example, two grades of care worker, to take account of some people having more experience and therefore more responsibility. Another situation is when both volunteers and paid staff, or part-time and full-time workers, tackle different aspects of a broad activity such as "provide support and care for users".

Managers will often want to keep an eye on situations like this to check if things are working out as planned or if they need to re-think matters. Other people outside the organisation may have questions, perhaps about the quality of the service (if some people are less skilled or experienced than others) or about the costs (if some people are paid more than others). In these circumstances the project may want to monitor what people are doing – how they spend their time, whether they are doing work on their own or if they are supervising or being supervised by someone else, etc.

The project

This situation arose in a day care centre for older people. It was based in a small town ("more of a big village") with a mix of paid and volunteer workers providing the direct service to the users. The paid workers were all there five days each week while the volunteers each did one or two days a week. This pattern had grown up over the years. Originally all the people involved were volunteers but as the members had become older and more frail the management committee decided to apply for funding with a few full-time paid staff with nursing or similar background. Seven years later the numbers of paid and volunteer workers on any day where about equal.

The people concerned were content with the way the service was organised. The paid staff concentrated on some tasks and the volunteers on others, but they gave each other a hand as necessary. However the Social Work Department and Health Board, which funded the project and whose staff referred most of the

L

users to the project, had expressed reservations about centres which had a mix of volunteers and paid staff. They asked this project, and others in the area, to consider whether they wanted to be a day centre with volunteers, catering for fitter older people and offering essentially social activities, or a day care centre, caring for frailer elderly people with all paid staff. This project felt that this division was wrong – it might be alright for the city but not for them. The committee's initial reaction was that they wanted to stay as they were "with the best of both worlds". However they had no real evidence to back this up. Also at the committee meeting where this was discussed some people expressed the view that perhaps there was some sense in the suggestion of the funders and that they ought to review the present arrangement – this matter had not been discussed fully since the original decision to apply for the salaried posts.

The committee decided to look first at what the volunteers and staff were doing to see how similar or different their activities and goals actually were. There were two reasons for tackling the matter in this way.

1. There was no pressure on the project to make a quick answer or to choose a particular direction. On checking it out, it turned out that the Health Board and Social Work Department were only seeking ideas and reactions at this stage.

2. They considered asking the users for their views, but decided it would be sensible to postpone this. They were anxious not to upset or worry users unnecessarily about the possibility of the service changing or of anyone leaving. They also wanted to be clearer about what they would ask the users, since, depending on how discussions went with the funders, this was something they might come back to.

What was done

The co-ordinator drew up a list of tasks which the staff and volunteers did. This was circulated to everyone who made suggestions about things she had missed or where they thought two items were really the same. After discussion, it was decided to include a long list of categories grouped under broad headings, as this was felt to be easier to manage. The revised list became the basis of the monitoring exercise.

The original plan was to use this for a week but it was decided to cover a fortnight to better reflect the input of the volunteers who only came one day each week ("one day to learn and another to get it right"). There was a sheet for each person to complete each day. As they went about their work they ticked off the appropriate category, with the most frequent activities getting lots of ticks as the day went on. Some people kept their sheet and a pencil in their pocket while others preferred to leave it in the office and mark off the things they had done every half an hour or so.

Inevitably, this caught the curiosity of the users. The project staff had not told the users about this beforehand, so the care workers had to explain. After that some users took it on themselves to remind the workers to fill in their forms.

At the end of the fortnight the co-ordinator gathered the sheets together and pulled the information together. She then prepared a list for the volunteers and another for the paid workers, showing the range of activities and how frequently various tasks had been marked (the total number of ticks). This showed that although both volunteers and paid workers had tackled a similar very wide range of activities over the course of the two weeks, they had mostly concentrated on different things.

How the information was used

Results were fed back to the workers first of all. If anything, they were mostly surprised that the exercise had confirmed that they were in fact doing broadly what they were supposed to be doing.

The management committee used this in a response to the Health Board and Social Work Department, arguing that neither group of workers could replace the other and that all the tasks were important. Other voluntary projects had made similar comments, although usually with no information to explain their views, so there was a lot of interest in this project's experience. Since then, some services to older people have been revised but this project is still continuing on the same basis as before.

The exercise did however raise other issues which the project then had to give some thought to. These included whether volunteers should go on more training courses and whether they needed to recruit more volunteers to allow the project to change the way some things were organised – for example giving more one-to-one contact with the users and having volunteers doing all of the bus escorts so other people could better respond to users' needs as they arrived in the morning.

Given the interest that had been shown in the completion of these lists, the project also fed back some information to the users. The level of interest in the actual findings was not particularly high – the consensus was that the users knew all along what the workers did. This information was kept very broad and no mention was made of the distinction between staff and volunteers, given the uncertainty about future arrangements at that stage.

Notes

The co-ordinator and other people agreed they ought to have explained to the users beforehand what was happening and why – both as a courtesy and to reassure people.

The volunteers and staff did find this stressful. They felt they had to be very busy and put in a great day's work, especially on the first day, even though they knew they were expected to just behave as usual. It was easier for the paid workers who got used to the form and relaxed more after the first few days. In this respect the decision to cover a fortnight rather than just a week was a good one.

In this case the co-ordinator noted how frequently activities were marked as well as the range. This could only be a rough estimate as most people acknowledged they did not bother to note every time they did something which occurred very frequently. Here, this level of accuracy was fine for the purposes of the exercise, and the limitation was made clear in the discussion with the funders. If you needed to know *exactly* how often each activity occurred you would have to think about how to build this in. On a related point, this monitoring exercise made no attempt to note the amount of time spent on each activity; one activity which took an hour and another taking two minutes each got a single tick. Again, this was made clear to the people being told the findings of the monitoring. The next case example shows how the time taken to do activities can be identified.

CASE EXAMPLE 18

Monitoring workers' activities: distribution of time

Background and Circumstances

The last case example showed how people working in a project identified the range of tasks they undertook.

Sometimes people are all too aware of what they are doing but are concerned about not having enough time to plan or think about future developments or the project overall ("being too busy to be able to do the job"). There may be tensions about how much time they spend on some tasks – whether too much or too little. Other typical problems are workers spending considerably more time with the project than their allocated hours in order to keep on top of the work and people feeling under stress.

In all these situations the first step in tackling the problem is to know how the time is really being spent. It is important to check this. Sometimes it feels as if a particular issue is dominating our working lives when in fact the problem is more of an irritation. Similarly, there can be tasks which we believe we have addressed regularly but which are not looked at for weeks on end.

The research method most commonly used to establish how people spent their time is a structured diary, and it was this method which was adopted in this study.

The Project

This project provided a wide range of services for ethnic minority families. It was based in a city centre and many families who used the project lived nearby. The main focus of the project was on children and parents, especially mothers, and elderly people, most of whom had little or no spoken English. The project aimed to provide advice and information and social care activities for users, such as Mother and Toddler groups and day care. It also sought to enable users to make appropriate use of other services, such as health care and education. For example, a project worker might go with a mother to hospital to give her encouragement and help in explaining and understanding about her child's illness. The project also sought to make these other agencies more aware of the needs and interests of ethnic minority people and families.

The project considered it important to link in to structures such as the local voluntary/statutory forum and other agencies concerned with the interests of people from ethnic minorities. However staff were concerned about the amount of time they were spending in these meetings, especially when the focus was on more general issues and not specific to their particular groups of users, since this left less time for direct contact with users.

The staff wanted to reconsider how they interacted with other voluntary and statutory agencies. It had been important to be at these meetings when the project was becoming established, but perhaps there were now better ways of dealing with this.

The staff were also very concerned about how often they were asked to undertake work by other agencies, rather than by users, and the types of requests. A particular issue was translating. The project staff felt that they were sometimes being used inappropriately for this, when the agency should have anticipated the difficulty and arranged for someone to translate when an appointment had been made with the person. However, to refuse to translate would have put the user to further embarrassment and inconvenience.

The project and its managers were planning to take up with the main statutory agencies the whole issue of how users accessed services and the role which the project should take in this. They therefore wanted more information about the frequency and scale of requests by agency staff to complement other information such as feedback from users.

What Was Done

The project staff drew up a list of their main activities. This was used as the basis of a diary which was kept for a fortnight. Each person filled out a sheet each day, marking it off as the day progressed.

At the end of this period the administrator worked out how much time had been spent by each person against the various categories from the original list. She then collated a combined one which showed the total frequency of events and time spent by the project as a whole on the various activities.

This confirms that a high proportion of time was spent by the co-ordinator in meetings, but the impact on the project overall was less marked as the other workers were less frequently involved. Similarly, the overall level of translating was less than expected, but was found to focus on one or two particular units. The results of the monitoring also highlighted the way some individuals were using the project (for example some people only raising matters at a crisis stage, others frequently returning with routine matters other than going direct to other services).

How the Information was Used

The project team and the management committee discussed the findings and how they could take on these issues. A plan was devised which would bring the project's pattern of work closer to what they considered appropriate at this stage. There were meetings with some other service providers about the role of the project. The project also looked at their hours of opening and how they could further encourage users to go direct to fuel boards etc, rather than automatically bringing problems to the project. They also decided that the two other project workers should take on some of the contacts with other voluntary groups to give the co-ordinator more time at the project and for planning and other management tasks.

Over the next six months or so the project gradually introduced these changes. The diary exercise was repeated about nine months after the original one and the results compared. This showed that some of the changes they were aiming at had occurred but other areas were still causing problems. After discussion, the project again decided to take steps, but this time to keep the progress under closer review.

Review of Existing Time Sheets

The project in the example above designed special sheets to monitor what they did. Many other projects already have time sheets. It is possible to use these, perhaps with some small changes, to meet other information needs.

One example was a project based in a rural area. Staff spent a considerable proportion of their time away from the office base, giving services to users or having contact with other services such as local schools. Staff filled in weekly time sheets, which showed were they had been. These had been designed to let managers deal with the need for flexible management arrangements, for example with staff working slightly more than their allotted hours one week and fewer the next.

Staff in this project were arguing for an increased travel budget. They thought that the evidence for this lay in their time sheets, which showed how they had to travel between meetings at different locations, sometimes doubling back on a journey later in the day. Over the course of a month the secretary drew up a list of all the places staff had visited and the reasons for these meetings etc. She also collated the total mileage done by all the project staff: this was not usually done, as each person submitted individual mileage claims. The co-ordinator then used this material in discussions with managers.

In the course of putting this information together and checking some additional points, the co-ordinator noted that the time sheets showed some other interesting points about how the project was functioning. For example, as in the case of the other project, staff were aware of the need to keep a balance between building good relations with other agencies, having face to face contact with users and doing other work on behalf of the users. She also noticed that there were some inconsistencies in how various workers described similar activities on their time sheets. The description was clear enough for the original purpose, but made it difficult for her to get an overall pattern of how the project was working.

This was discussed at one of the Team's regular meetings. Staff decided to keep using the existing timesheets – which had to be completed anyway – but to use consistent descriptions over activities, which they agreed at the meeting. At the end of three months the co-ordinator and secretary brought the information together from these sheets. Again, they did a list for each person and then for the project overall, showing the distribution of time over different activities and over different locations. The team then used this for their own planning about how to move on from the initial phase of getting the project established into a more settled way of working. They also used back up material from this to further back up the case for the increased travel budget, which they successfully secured for the next financial year.

Notes

As can be seen from the first project, monitoring activities will itself not solve the problems facing a project concerning how time is spent or the need for working overtime. This is only the first stage and has to be followed up by planning steps which will put matters right. It is also important to monitor whether or not these measures have any effect. This can either be done by repeating a specific diary exercise, as with the first project, or using an on-going monitoring system, which is what the second project had effectively established.

Monitoring exercises of this sort can also be expanded to identify the skills and knowledge needed to do the tasks. This could be added in an extra column to the diary sheets. This would enable the project to look at whether people needed specialist knowledge of a subject when teaching other people or giving advice, the use of counselling skills etc. This information could be used to consider training needs, either for existing staff or when planning to recruit new staff or volunteers.

ACTIVITIES DIARY

DATE: Initials:

Activity	Time spent	User	With whom	Where	Reason/s	Professional input
eg meeting, interview, phone call	5/10/15 mins, then to nearest 15 min	name of users or note of group this task was for	eg user, teachers, doctors, Gas Board	eg office, hospital, person's home	eg admin, health care, debt	eg interpreting, counselling, give information, negotiating etc.

7

Planning for new services: Feasibility Study

WHY THIS NEEDS TO BE DONE

Most of us can spend a good deal of time and effort considering what to do about an idea about something we have not tried before: we are not sure how to go about it, we don't know if it will work or if we will like it. Our choices are to leave well alone and stick with what we know, go all out and do the new thing, or try it in a small way or in a way that does not wholly commit us. To take a fairly mundane example of decoration in our homes, if you have a hankering to change the livingroom from co-ordinated neutrals to bright clashing reds and greens, you can either sit down and wait till the notion passes, go ahead and change everything or try it somewhere, for example painting the patch of wall behind the settee, borrow red curtains or a sheet from a friend and such like.

Which course you take depends on:

- whether it will be possible to put it back or disentangle the situation if it doesn't work out;
- how expensive and inconvenient it will be to do it and then change it back if necessary;
- what you know about the details of how it can be put into effect or how it will work;
- what the consequences will be for you and other people if you do it; and
- what the consequences will be if you *don't* do it.

To take our example of changing the furnishings in a room, the main factor is probably the cost. Cutting down mature trees to build a garage, on the other hand, involves a more complex consideration of all these factors.

Planning for the future in a voluntary organisation is much the same, especially when planning new services or considering substantial changes to existing ones. Sometimes the need is quite clear, we already know how to deliver the service (or someone else is available to show us) and it can be met out of existing resources. Other times the decision to proceed is less clear-cut. We know there is a need for something else but we are not sure exactly what. Someone in the Committee is advocating strongly for a new service, but is there a widespread need or will it be used only by a few people? Making the changes may involve a lot of inconvenience to you and especially the users, so you do not want to do this unless you have good reason to think the new plans will work.

Sometimes it is possible to operate the new service or the change to the existing one for a few months on a trial basis – what is sometimes called a "pilot". This would give you time to find if the new idea can work, discover most of the teething problems and plan any refinements you would want to make. If you do decide to continue, the experience will give you the basis for an application to funders as a separate project or tied into your overall activities. You will need to monitor and evaluate this pilot scheme carefully, drawing on the various types of information gathering discussed in the earlier sections of this handbook, such as charting the scale of use and the views of users.

There are other situations, however, when you need information at an even earlier stage: to find out if the idea is feasible at all. This involves finding out in as much detail as possible such points as:

- the likely scale of use of your proposed service;
- the kinds of people who would use it, and in what ways;
- what it is hoped the users would gain from the service; and
- what needs it would address.

When doing a feasibility study we are evaluating an idea, rather than an existing service. It is important to remember we are not just looking for evidence to back up a decision we have already made. We need to keep an open mind that our original premise may not be borne out, and that our plans can be changed and improved upon. This is a good way of involving potential users from the beginning and as with other parts of monitoring and evaluation there is not much point in asking people to contribute if we do not then listen to what they say. We may not do exactly what people suggest: it could be that a lot of people want us to do one thing but the evidence shows that a small group with greater needs would benefit from something else. We then have to make a decision about which way to go, but at least it is an informed decision.

Once you have gathered information and reassessed your plans you have to take decisions. Again this can mean going ahead, putting the idea aside as not feasible, trying it out on a small scale or getting still more information.

CASE EXAMPLES

The 2 case examples here have situations where projects were being encouraged to introduce a new service or an additional part to an existing service, but wanted more information about the likely demand. As it happens, at the end of the day the findings from these feasibility studies in both cases led to the organisation changing these plans.

In both these cases the project did not know who their potential users were, so they were gathering information mostly from professionals. In other circumstances, where an organisation does know that a new service will be used mostly by existing members or by a group of people who can be identified fairly easily, it would be possible to ask the potential users for their views, for example by a survey of the kind described in Section 4.

CASE EXAMPLE 19

Potential use of a service: monitoring enquiries

Background and Circumstances

Many people in voluntary organisations providing direct social care services are aware that there are people in their area who would like to use the service and would benefit from it, but there are no spare places which the project can offer. Because other professionals know of the heavy demand on the project they do not make referrals. Similarly, if a project also takes direct requests from users, their family and friends and such like, the project usually stops publicising the service when demand is high. This makes life a bit easier to manage for the project. However it can also make it harder to demonstrate the extent of the unmet demand as the waiting list or list of unmet requests will be an under-estimate of the real problem.

This is a very typical example of how monitoring and evaluation can help plan for the services which might be provided. The overall aim beside which anything will be measured is still known from the outset. This is to provide the service which best meets the needs of people with particular characteristics living in this area.

The Project

This was a day care centre for older people situated in a medium-sized town. It took referrals from professionals, such as social workers, home helps, GPs and community nursing staff, and directly from older people and their families and friends. Frequently existing members of the day centre asked if a neighbour or friend could come and in this way the project had learned of vulnerable people who were not known to the statutory service network. The centre had been operating for six years and after the first year or so all its places had been taken. There was a waiting list and new referrals could only have a place when someone left. The centre already had a waiting list and details of all outstanding formal referrals were known, but the co-ordinators and volunteers knew that this was only the tip of the iceberg.

Plans to expand the service had been discussed a few years ago but were postponed because there had been difficulties recruiting and keeping enough volunteers. This problem had settled down and there was now a good-sized group of experienced, confident volunteers. Although the project covered all of the town it was located near the main shopping street which was on the east side of the town, near the old harbour. It had been suggested that an offshoot be opened in a church hall further up the hill on the west side since there were no community facilities for elderly people in that area and some elderly people were known to have problems getting into town.

The day care centre was now hoping to expand to another location and/or open another day each week. Before it took matters further the committee decided to explore the extent of unmet demand to help make the case for additional funding.

What was done

The project kept a note of all requests for services. This included enquiries about whether they could take a specific person or if an existing member could come more often, or if there were likely to be any spaces, whether for elderly people in general or for specific individuals. This was recorded in a notebook with columns drawn down the page for:

- the date;
- who made the request (user, member of the public, home help organiser, etc);
- whether the request was about a specific person or more general;
- the location of the potential user if this was known, and especially whether it was in the proposed new area; and
- any other relevant notes, for example if the person was looking for a place two days a week, needed wheelchair access, etc.

The notebook was kept in the office beside the phone. It was expected that the people who would be most affected would be the co-ordinator, the part-time administrator/secretary and the Chair of the management committee, but all the volunteer care workers and other committee members knew of the monitoring. In the event, over half these people were also approached – mostly with fairly general enquiries about the spare places. People also received requests in informal ways outside the centre and office. These were also noted down as soon as possible in the notebook. Some of these very informal requests were missed, but the people involved were confident that almost all the information they were seeking was recorded.

At the end of the month the information was analysed by the co-ordinator and the Chair of the management committee. The points they looked at were:

- total number of requests;

- how many of these came from users and the public and how many from professionals; and
- the demand for service in the planned new location.

This exercise showed that the potential demand for the service was indeed much higher than the number of formal referrals suggested. Members of the public and users made enquiries for specific elderly people – usually relatives and neighbours. The professionals were as likely to make general enquiries as to ask about a place for a particular person. Perhaps most importantly for purposes of this particular monitoring exercise, the demand for additional days or places at the existing location was found to be higher than the demand for a service at the new location.

The organisation then decided to feed back the results of this review to local professionals and community leaders such as clergymen, especially those who had made particular requests. They linked this to requests for more detailed information. This follow-up was done in a way very similar to the survey in the next case example, although the people were sent a shorter list of questions.

The replies to this second phase of the feasibility study confirmed the higher demand for the existing location. The centre managers therefore decided to concentrate their efforts on expanding the existing service and to look at more flexible transport arrangements for people in the outlying parts of the town.

Notes

This project used the monitoring of enquiries about the service to identify the overall level of demand. It was still based on people raising the matter with the project and so could not be as thorough or as accurate as a survey of all potential referrals which had a good response rate. However this type of monitoring exercise is quite simple and places little demands on project staff and no extra demands on any other people. It is therefore a good starting point, especially for any existing service which takes referrals from a wide range of formal and informal routes.

CASE EXAMPLE 20

Survey of potential referrers

Background and Circumstances

This case example takes up at the point where the preliminary monitoring of enquiries stops.

One way of looking at the gap between the potential users and the potential service is to start by firming up the idea of the service and then finding out who might use it. The other approach is to firm up the picture of the people and find out what kind of service or options they would like.

In each situation we are moving towards a clearer picture of both the users and the service or project, since in both cases we are using the response to our initial idea to reassess that idea.

In the last case example the group began with an idea in the minds of potential users and referrers about the kind of service the project would provide – essentially an extension or repeat of the existing day care centre. This was sensible in this case – this voluntary organisation was familiar with this type of activity but would have been less confident about branching out in a new direction. In other situations, however, it is possible to start with a clean slate.

The Project

Unlike the other case examples in this handbook, this did not involve an existing project, but rather grew out of the work of several projects and an existing voluntary organisation. The organisation had several projects working with teenagers within a Local Authority Region. The project in one location had been asked to take referrals similar to those dealt with by the project in another town, which gave a specialist service to children of secondary school age who were having a disrupted education.

The voluntary organisation followed this up and began discussions with the Education and Social Work Departments about these referrals and whether they could be accommodated within the existing project or dealt with in some other way. This was a fairly wide-ranging discussion about ways of complementing existing and planned provision for this group of children. The local authority had also been aware of a gap in the services available, and were planning to tackle this in a particular way. They suspected this would only solve part of the problem, but could not quite put their finger on where the remaining problems would be or how best to tackle them.

In order to better assess the level and type of needs for some kind of service, it was agreed to carry out a short feasibility study. This could then be considered alongside other information about the use and demand for existing services.

What was done

A form was drawn up which incorporated the main points of information already identified as relevant by a planning group, which consisted of a manager from the voluntary organisation and key people from the relevant local authority departments. Copies of these were sent to the headteacher of each school with secondary provision in this area, with the suggestion that guidance staff participated in the exercise. The scope of the survey was intentionally kept very wide. Staff were asked to complete a form for each child who was currently (or recently) receiving substantial extra support or care from the education or social work system, or who was giving concern and who might benefit from some extra support.

An unexpectedly high number of children were identified by this exercise. Some needed only a small level of extra support while others were children with complex problems. The ages of these children and the type of extra input which they needed was quite different from that suggested by the original enquiries to the existing project and from the current caseloads of the local authority staff. The younger children and those with the most severe problems were going to be catered for by the planned improvements which were going to be brought in by the local authority departments later that year. However the main gap was for children in third and fourth years of secondary education who were beginning to drift away from school, largely because they were bored and under-achieving, and who were then getting into trouble. The voluntary organisation and the Education Department then began looking at ways in which a project could have a base both inside and outside schools, working with classroom and guidance teachers to provide these young people with relevant education that would be of interest and of value to them, perhaps linking in to local employers and other voluntary interests.

Notes

The planning group were fairly confident that the headteachers themselves would not have the information which was needed. The problem was that they wanted to reach the guidance teachers, but knew that a few headteachers might be offended if the formal request did not come to them. The suggestion in the letter that guidance teachers be involved was a way of trying to tackle this. This kind of situation arises quite often when surveys are sent to large organisations. Another approach is to send a copy to the people you really want to complete the schedule, with another copy sent to the person in charge so that they are kept informed. If anything, requests for information of this type are more difficult than usual: in a school setting, if the planning group had sent requests for information about already identified children they could easily have been passed to the appropriate teacher within the school. However asking about children who fitted a certain type or characteristic posed more of a problem.

The number of forms returned from the various schools varied widely, when account was taken of the size of the school rolls. This could have been a result of different people interpreting the definition differently, of being more aware of children in their school who were having problems coping, or the level of interest shown in the exercise by the people concerned. For all these reasons, the planning group were fairly confident that there were more children within schools in this area who could benefit from a project of this type. However the estimate was very useful for their planning purposes, as they could be fairly confident that if a project were provided the schools which had made more returns were likely to be those to initially refer children to them. The project was likely to start in some schools and spread out to others, and this helped them plan where would be the best places to start.

FEASIBILITY STUDY

Pupil's Name:

Date of Birth: Male/Female

School: S1/S2/S3/S4

Address: [street and town]

STATUS   Mark any known of:

	current	previous		current	previous
Guidance	☐	☐	List D	☐	☐
School Behaviour Support	☐	☐	List G: residential	☐	☐
EBSS: in school	☐	☐	day:	☐	☐
out of school	☐	☐	Statutory sw orders	☐	☐
mix	☐	☐			
Education Social Work	☐	☐	Referral to Reporter	☐	☐

Main Reason For Identifying Child:

General Demeanour Please note any relevant points under each of the following headings:

Behaviour in class

School attendance

Relationship with teachers

Relationship with peers

Family circumstances

Educational attainment

Any learning difficulties; health problems

What type of provision would you find useful for pupils like this child?

Any specific outcomes you would want to see achieved:

THANK YOU FOR YOUR HELP
Please return this form to:

PART THREE:
PUTTING IT ALL TOGETHER

1

Points of Information which Funders Need

The following list covers points of information which the fieldwork for this study identified as being useful to most voluntary organisations. It is based on:

- the experience of the projects participating in the fieldwork, including those commenting on the approach and findings;

- the experience and feedback gained from other organisations with whom those projects were working, especially their funders and referrers; and

- the requirements of the local authority Social Work Departments and other funding agencies covered by the survey.

Each voluntary organisation needs to develop a system which will cover information which is relevant to the details and circumstances of that project. For example, timescales will vary: some projects will only need to have information about the use made of their service on an annual basis, while others will want information about levels of use over much shorter periods. This list is only a general guide and in each case it will be helpful to clarify the requirements with funders and referrers. It also should be borne in mind that it is not necessary to gather all the information listed here on a continual basis: this is discussed in greater detail in the Handbook.

Scale of Activities

Level of use at each session, for example, number of enquiries or visitors.

Total level of service given in a week/month/quarter/year, for example, day care days, home care hours, visits to information centre, etc.

The level of service at particular times of the day/week/month/year if this can fluctuate.

Total number of *users* over a month/quarter/year, to take account of situations where people make repeated use of the service. This will be more important if the project is providing services over a long period, such as community care projects, than for projects designed for one-off contacts.

Number of people joining the service, with a distinction between people coming for the first time and those returning after a break if this is relevant.

Number of people leaving the service, if relevant.

Characteristics of Users

Age: broad bands for general public, smaller bands or by year for services aimed at specific groups.

Gender

Area or address where this is relevant: this could be very wide, such as local authority region or district or very specific such as street, estate or village. Also note whether people are within or outside any catchment or target area.

Any particular characteristics relevant to your project, for example wheelchair use or other limited mobility, sight or hearing disabilities, person living alonetc.

For each characteristic, whether it exists, and the severity if this is relevant and identifiable.

How Users Reached the Project

How they heard of the project, who suggested or referred them to this.

Why they came to you or were referred.

Use by Individual People (NB: especially important for community care projects)
Frequency or extent of use of:
- main service
- additional or special activities
- individual care
- any special arrangements not normally part of the project
- use of other activities run by other organisations arranged by or through the project.

Practical Aspects
Use of premises, transport, catering etc:
- scale of any special demands or arrangements

- scale and nature of any problems caused for users or project
- any other records needed for the project's own management or budgeting, such as rotas for transport escort.

Outcomes for Users (NB: especially important for community care services)

Whether the main purposes in the user coming to the project were met – both positive changes and the absence or reduction of undesirable factors.

Any other intended outcomes.

Any relevant unintended outcomes.

Outcomes for indirect users, such as carers of the frail or disabled people, other members of the user's family.

Outcomes for the whole community.

Outcomes for Other Services (NB: especially important for community care services)

Impact of services given to individual users or by project overall on relevant other voluntary or statutory services:
- scale or levels of their services
- quality of care given to users
- role of care staff.

Feedback from Users

Their views and experiences of the service:
- elements they find useful
- elements they do not find useful
- usefulness of information provided about and by project
- convenience of location, times available, access etc
- aspects they like and dislike
- what changes they would make to existing activities
- new services or activities they would add.

Use and experiences of different types of users – for example with different characteristics, those referred or self-initiated.

Views and experiences of people using the project in different ways, for example the main service only or also using additional activities.

Feedback From Other Services
- usefulness of project to them
- usefulness of project to shared clients.

Staffing and Volunteers

Number of staff, including whole-time equivalent if part-time staff are involved.

Number of volunteers.

Levels of cover over different times.

Input to main activities.

Record of volunteer recruitment arrangements and outcome in numbers recruited.

Finances

Income from different sources, for example, grants, fees, donations, general fundraising, sales, etc.

Expenditure on different items such as staff salaries and related costs, volunteer expenses, training, rent etc: these are usually listed out on the application form. A note of how these have varied from the estimates or budgets made at the beginning of the year.

Expenditure on each main activity (for example day care, information service, etc), taking account of staff and volunteer time in preparation and follow-up and, where appropriate, a proportion of management and overhead costs.

Expenditure on each group of users or individual user, especially for some community care projects.

2

Steps to make Monitoring and Evaluation Easier

MANAGERS (MANAGEMENT COMMITTEES, SENIOR MANAGERS)

The experience of the projects who helped develop these monitoring and evaluation methods showed that there were practical steps which can make these tasks easier or more complicated. The following suggestions apply to all types of settings and types of monitoring or evaluation activities.

Make sure there are clear aims and objectives for the project and that staff know what is expected of them.

Set the overall framework and context for monitoring and evaluation work, as part of your responsibility for overall planning and development and for ensuring a good quality of services.

Ensure that monitoring and evaluation is being done for each level as appropriate: overall planning, specific activities, services for users.

Encourage staff to plan monitoring and evaluation work properly and put it in the context of other work, rather than rushing into it or tagging it on as an afterthought.

Make sure that appropriate people outside the project (especially funders and referrers) are kept informed of plans and progress as necessary.

Be ready to get involved in planning the monitoring and evaluation work with the project, but keep an open mind as this may not always be appropriate.

Provide additional management support if this is needed while the project is doing monitoring and evaluation work.

Be ready to deal with any problems and issues that the monitoring and evaluation highlight in a positive way.

Realise that change might be necessary and that there may be criticisms of the service. Encourage staff to regard this positively.

Think of ways of giving practical help to the project, such as a loan of extra administrative cover, someone to "baby-sit" the project while staff have meetings to plan the work or discuss the results and implications.

Make sure someone takes on the role of "progress chaser" and keeps the monitoring and evaluation work on track. If the work falls behind schedule revise the plan and timescale.

Check that the project's plans and targets for the monitoring and evaluation work are reasonable and achievable. Start discussions with funders if they have unreasonable expectations.

Think about how to make the best use of the information gathered and the findings. This is not just for the annual report to funders: it can also help in other ways such as volunteer recruitment and training, publicity, planning longer-term developments.

If you have several funders and referrers who ask for information in different ways approach them to see if a single or shared format can be agreed.

Staff, Including Co-ordinators

Keep an open mind. Be willing to accept criticisms and to accept that change and improvement may be need.

Check what other people are expecting of you in doing the monitoring and evaluation work and tell them if this is not realistic. Also check their timescales and the format they would prefer for statistics, reports etc.

Think about how the team can get involved in the process.

Be flexible about who does which tasks. Build on people's experiences and skills and work towards developing these in other people, so you do not become too dependant on a few individuals.

Recognise that monitoring and evaluation work will be an additional demand in the short-term, but that it becomes easier once it is established. Think of ways of integrating arrangements with other day-to-day work and making it routine. Also think of how you will balance demands from other work, especially the service to users.

Think about how you feed back information to the people who helped provide it, such as users, local professionals in other agencies etc. They are more likely to go on being helpful if you thank and involve them.

Funders and Referrers

Make sure projects know what you expect of them:

- that there is an agreed remit;

- your expectations on scale of activities, quality of service etc are put as clearly as possible;
- that your records are kept updated on any agreed changes.

Be willing to get involved in the planning stage for monitoring and evaluation work when necessary and appropriate.

Accept that changes to the project may be needed and that comments to projects may be critical of your services. Respond positively to projects when they raise matters highlighted by the monitoring and evaluation.

Be realistic and sensible in what you expect projects' evaluations to achieve. Be willing to consider revising timescales or expectations if circumstances change – for example if there are staff illnesses.

Consider how much flexibility you can give projects on the presentation of information to you. Remember that not all organisations will be able to gather information the same way, but that this is still reliable.

Bear in mind that your own internal organisational changes – restructuring, staff changes, revised referral criteria – can have far-reaching effects on many aspects of voluntary organisations' work, including the monitoring and evaluation of their activities (against changing criteria or timescales).

Recognise that monitoring and evaluation tasks are an additional demand on projects, especially in the early stages when the system is not yet routine and when preparing reports. Avoid overloading staff unnecessarily.

Consider how you can give practical help to projects, such as a loan of extra administrative staff, advice about and/or access to computers, help with getting reports typed and copied. An input of special expertise on monitoring and evaluation, or additional funds to buy this in, will be very useful in some circumstances.

Disseminate ideas for monitoring and evaluation and how to do it to other projects.

Respond to projects' annual reports and other forms of feedback. Tell them what was useful or successful – on their achievements and in the feedback itself – and what you would like changed.

Make sure that your representatives on project management and advisory groups know what their role is and when they should be passing information back to colleagues in the local office or Headquarters.

If at all possible, you should ensure each voluntary organisation with whom you are working (funding or providing related services) is given an identified liaison person who can advise the voluntary organisation and act as channel for communication with other parts of the agency.

Review the way your grants administration, policy development and care management sections function and the internal communication arrangements to ensure that you gain maximum benefit from feedback by voluntary organisations and unnecessary burdens are not being placed on them.

Consider how your information requirements interact with those of other funders or referrers. If you jointly fund projects with another funder (for example, a Social Work Department and Health Board) explore ways of meeting both needs on a single timetable and format and against a joint list of conditions and criteria. Another option is to have a reduced level of detailed feedback from groups which receive only a part of their funding from you.

3
Writing a report

No matter how good the quality and completeness of the information that you have gathered about your project, and how relevant and useful this will be for your Committee, the main way in which it will have an impact is when it is written up in some kind of report or document that can be copied and passed on to other people. For many people this is the biggest headache of all. This section therefore gives some ideas on how to tackle this in a way that will be easy for you.

There are seven stages to writing a report and each one of them contributes to make the overall task as easy and productive as possible:

1. do the initial planning;
2. do an outline;
3. gather the information together;
4. start writing the report;
5. revise the first draft;
6. prepare the final version; and
7. distribute it to the people who need to receive the report.

1. The Initial Planning

It is a good idea to start the whole process as early as possible – long, long before the actual deadline for submission of the report. The first thing is to make a plan before you start putting pen to paper at all. Think about:

* Who is the report for?
* What do they want to know?
* What do you want to tell them?

These are the kind of things you can think about as you are doing the washing up or going to work in the morning. Once you have had a ponder list all this out. Be honest with yourself – after all this is only your own working notes.

Thinking through what the report is going to address often highlights some of the common problems that people experience with reports. One of these is mixed audiences. Often reports are being aimed at several different types of people: the project committee, funders, other people in local authorities, other workers in the project, the users, the wider public in your area, other voluntary groups. Sometimes there is one main audience. However at other times it is a bit more complicated than this. It is a good idea to list this out for each of the various audiences. Then look at the lists. If there is a large overlap between their interests, you will probably be alright in having one main report. However, if there is very little overlap it might be more sensible just to plan from the outset to do two separate reports. If you do decide to do two reports, it is usually easier to do the longer report first – for example for the committee and the main funder – with a summary or another version focusing on one particular aspect for another funder or for other voluntary groups. Another approach is to have

annexes – for example a main report for general distribution, with a detailed financial part in an annex for the funder.

Another very common problem is not being sure what your audience wants to know. The best thing is to ask the people concerned what it is they want to know. However you may not think this appropriate or possible at this early stage, so you can use another list which covers the most usual interests. The one suggested at Section 2 of this part of the Handbook will be helpful here.

2. Prepare the Outline

Once you have thought through what the report is going to be about, you can then prepare an outline of the report. This would have section headings and perhaps a very brief note of any points you particularly want emphasised under each heading. An example of a possible outline is attached at the end of this section. Your outline would probably look a bit like this, but with a few notes or phrases under some of the headings.

Once you have your outline, this is usually the stage to discuss it with other people, such as your liaison/contact person in the local authority. It is much easier to make changes and to add or omit things at this stage, rather than when you have got a neatly typed report.

Once you are happy, list out and note what you want to cover in each section. Then list out what information you need and where you will get it. The list at Section 2 is a long detailed version of what you will need. You will probably have a shorter list. It is then a good idea to mark off another column or write in beside each item where the information will come from. If you did the planning day (see Section 1 of Part 2) and still have your notes from this they will be very useful here. You could also draw up a special list with a "to do" and "information received" columns. This could be pinned to the wall or kept on your desk. This is especially useful if the circumstances of your project mean that you have to do a lot of chasing up of other people. Again, an idea of how this might look is attached to the end of the Section.

3. Gather the information together

This is the stage when you gather in last year's report, notes from people who are running related parts of the project, collect the information from the records etc. Do any analysis that is still needed: this is discussed in more detail at Section 4 of this part of the handbook. Also prepare any charts or tables you want to use, for example to summarise how many users are in different age groups, or to show the differences between this year and last year.

Don't assume you have to do all this yourself, even if you are the person who is going to be writing the report. You might be able to get other people to gather the information together for certain parts. For example a day-care centre that also has a befriending scheme and a home support scheme might want to get a volunteer or key worker from each of these to pull together their own information and pass it on to you.

4. Start writing the Report

Once you have the bits of information gathered together, or at least on their way to you, you can start writing. It is not necessary to write all the sections in the order that they will come in the final report – you can write them in any order if this is easier for you. (Personally, I usually leave the introduction as well as the conclusions to the end.)

One advantage of writing your report up in sections is that if you get stuck you can leave one part aside and then come back to it later. If you get stuck with the whole thing, put it aside for a few days and then come back to it fresh – it usually seems much more straightforward after a break.

It is a good idea to keep a notepad with you as you work for ideas or for points that you want to tie in with other sections or in the conclusions.

If you find it difficult to get peace to concentrate or enough space in the office, consider writing the report somewhere else. Think about your own organisation and its premises – what you are looking for is a large space to spread out papers, a table to write at and no telephone. Could you put a cover on the pool table for the papers and work at a card table when the games room is not being used? Is there a committee or conference room which is sometimes free? Some people can arrange a day working at home, or can work on the report in the evenings, although this is not always convenient. Another option might be to borrow a room or even a desk from another voluntary organisation, such as a youth club who use their premises mainly in the evenings.

5. Revise the First Draft

Once you have got all the sections together this is what is sometimes called the "first draft" stage: it is the first time you have a complete report, but it still needs some work done on it. It helps if you can leave it for a week or so before doing any further revision. Then come back and if possible read it all of apiece.

How is the length? The report only has to be as short as it needs to be, and it is more important that it is clear than that it is particularly long or short.

Think again about who the report is going to. Are these people going to be looking for something long and detailed with the full history of your organisation from the day it began 20 years ago, or do they want something that is quick and easy to read and covers the main points of your achievement in the last year? Both of these documents have their place, you just want to be sure that this is the right place for whatever you are writing.

Does the report flow together? Sometimes there are bumpy bits as one section moves into the next, with some points being repeated and others missed.

Is it saying what you want? Sometimes all the facts are there, but the overall emphasis is wrong – for example when you have highlighted all of the problems, but have forgotten to say how much fun the project is and how positive the users and workers feel about the achievements.

You may well want to have a second opinion and you might need to check that someone else is content – for example the Chair of the management committee. Make any changes that are needed. Once you are happy with it, you can go on to the next stage.

6. Preparing the Final Version

By now you have the content of the report right and it is saying what you want it to say. However you also want to make a good impression and the presentation is as important as the content.

Check the report over carefully. Check it for spelling and punctuation etc. Reading a document for spelling and style is different from reading it for content and meaning. Many people find it difficult to separate the two out in their mind, especially when they feel quite close to the whole exercise. This is the point when any friends or family who offered to do anything they could to help should get taken up on their offer and roped in. If you have a word processor which has a spell check you can also use this. If you have to check it yourself, one way is to do it with a ruler, looking at one line at a time and checking in the dictionary anything you are not certain about.

Also check the report carefully for the numbers – do the numbers in the tables and the graphs and the text all tie up? There may be discrepancies, in which case you have to explain this. For example, information might have come from different sources at different times of the year, or one figure might be the total

N

number of enquiries and the other is the total number of people who went on to use the service. The difference may have been very obvious to you when you were gathering the information together, but it may make other people confused or even have doubts about the project.

Once all the fine points are dealt with, get the report typed or printed for the finished version. Have a think about the typeface – is it a good enough size and is it dark enough? Remember that the document will probably be photocopied several times. If your word processor can only do a "draft" print, check if there are any other ways of printing it off such as using someone else's printer if this is compatible, or maybe even going to a commercial copy/print shop if this is a particularly important report for you.

7. Sending the Report out

If possible, get enough copies for all the people who need to see the report to be sent one copy each. The research study showed that staff in local authority departments and the like did not always pass reports from voluntary organisations on to colleagues. You might want to phone round and ask who needs copies of your report so that you can send them direct.

Send out a covering letter with the reports explaining why you have sent it and what the report is for – for example an annual report for funding, a mid-year report for discussion, a report on your evaluation, etc. It is a good idea to do this even if this is also covered in the text.

8. After the excitement

Have something to drink. Thank all the people who helped you and show them a copy of the final version. Tell yourself "well done". Then get back to all the rest of the work.

SUGGESTED REPORT OUTLINE

Introduction and Aims of Organisation

What this report is and who it is for.

Aims and Objectives: what is the organisation trying to achieve and how it does this.

This should be stated as clearly and as briefly as possible – do not just refer to or repeat your formal constitution.

Expand on this if necessary – for example, if you were set up to do three things and have decided to concentrate on two, note why and when this was decided by the committee and agreed with funders, referrers, etc.

Organisation of the service or group

Note the structure – a "map" is often useful, for example:-

Structure of Befriending Scheme

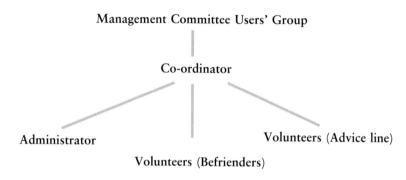

The numbers of co-ordinators, office staff, paid or volunteer workers etc.

Any relevant issues, such as unusually high volunteer turnover and recruitment.

Management arrangements: committee meetings, staff and volunteer meetings etc.

Activities

List out what the organisation or project does, including the main or core activities and any specific projects. Explain briefly what each involves and where it happens.

For example, for a befriending scheme this would cover:

- co-ordinate scheme by recruiting volunteers, matching to new users and providing continuing management and support;
- the range of befrienders' activities with the users;
- other aspects of the project such as advice or counselling to relatives.

How the service has been used

Scale of use.

Characteristics of users: for example, age, location, etc of individuals, types of other voluntary organisations.

Benefits gained

By main users.

By carers or other family members (if relevant).

By volunteers (if relevant – for example if one of the project's aims is to enable people to gain certain skills or experience through volunteering).

Contact with other agencies

Arrangements for referrals and ongoing liaison.

Benefits gained by them.

Practical matters

Any issues you want to raise about transport, premises, etc.

Financing of the organisation or service

A brief statement of total income, a list of the main sources, and also a note of any contributions in kind (for example, loan of local authority minibus, secondment of an additional worker).

Total expenditure.

Any notable changes from last year which make comparisons difficult or inappropriate. For example, if you have just recruited substantial numbers of volunteers the training costs and volunteers' expenses will be higher.

Conclusion

Summary of main points.

Discussion of issues.

A note of your future plans.

Annexes

Membership of management committee.

Detailed accounts, with notes on how these relate to your activities. Any points you want to explain, for example if your project has a couple of self-contained parts, or is carrying forward money from last year.

REPORT OUTLINE AND PLAN FOR GATHERING INFORMATION

Introduction	*Information From*
Aims and Objectives	Last year's report and Committee
Main changes during last year	minutes
Activities	
Range of activities	Diary monthly reports to
	Committee (Sue to look out)
Scale of Use and Characteristics	
of Users	Referral Forms:
Befrienders' scheme	Get from Mary
Advice Line	Get from Jim
Benefits gained	
By users	Survey done in summer,
	case notes from volunteers.
Finances	Last year's budget monthly
	forms etc (Sue to look out)

O

4

Analysing the information

COUNTING THINGS

Y ou can either start with each person (or record or case) on its own card or sheet, as was done in Case Examples 3 and 7 or have each item listed out, for example on a record book or a large sheet of paper.

It is a good idea to start by checking the total number of cases first, so people will be able to know if you have miscounted when things get more complicated later on. Depending on the numbers involved and how these are laid out, you can just add them up or note on a pad in fives (卌 ||).

To do a characteristic like age, gender etc, it is a good idea to list out the categories on a sheet of paper in the way of the table below, and then mark off each case or record as you go through them. It is a good idea to keep a note of the finished table in this form, even if you do not intend to use it this way in the report, as it will be easier for you to refer back to as working notes.

AGE OF USERS

Age of Users	Number	Percent
Under 18	40	20
18-44	60	30
45-59	50	25
60 and over	30	15
Not recorded	20	10
Total	200	100

To do a cross-table of two items, separate the cards or count up the appropriate records on the sheet according to one item, for example the gender. If you have cards, the easiest thing is to physically divide the cards according to the variables in the first item, for example dividing them into male and female. You then count out the other item, in this case age, in the same way as before. Doing cross-tables from record sheets is more difficult. Probably the easiest way is to mark out the layout of the table on a large sheet of paper and check through each record and mark it in the appropriate box using the 5 bar gate system. The numbers should then look like the table below.

Age	Female	Male
Under 18	‖‖‖ ‖‖‖ ‖	‖‖‖ ‖‖‖
18–44	‖‖‖ ‖‖‖ ‖‖‖	‖‖‖ ‖‖‖ ‖‖
45–59	‖‖‖ ‖‖‖ ‖‖‖ ‖‖‖ ‖‖	‖‖‖ ‖‖‖
60 and over	‖‖‖ ‖‖‖	‖‖‖ ‖‖‖

GENDER AND AGE OF USERS

Age of User	Female	(%)	Male	(%)	Total	(%)
Under 18	20	(50%)	20	(50%)	40	(100%)
18-44	20	(33%)	40	(67%)	60	(100%)
45-49	35	(70%)	15	(30%)	50	(100%)
60 and over	35	(70%)	15	(30%)	50	(100%)
	———		———		———	
All Ages	110	(55%)	90	(45%)	200	(100%)

OR

Age of User	Female	(%)	Male	(%)	Total	(%)
Under 18	20	(18.2%)	20	(22.2%)	40	(20%)
18-44	20	(18.2%)	40	(44.4%)	60	(30%)
45-59	35	(31.8%)	15	(16.7%)	50	(25%)
60 and over	35	(31.8%)	15	(16.7%)	50	(25%)
	———		———		———	
	110	(100.0%)	90	(100.0%)	200	(100%)

You then need to work out what percentages are most useful to you. You can go across the rows, which in this case means working out the percentage of males and females in each age group. Alternatively, you can go down the columns, which in this case would let you compare the age profile of men and women using the project.

GENDER AND AGE OF USERS

Age of User	Female	Male	Total
Under 18	20	20	40
18-44	20	40	60
45-59	35	15	50
over 60	35	15	50
Total	110	90	200

When there are several choices, for example when people could have several reasons for coming to a project, the easiest thing is to count by using 5-bar gates as before, marking off the several answers for each person before going on to the next. Another way is to count everyone for one answer, and then go all the way through everyone for the next. This will then look like the table below.

Here, because people can have more than one reason, this would add up to more than 200. We are interested in what percentage of all users gave each reason, so we take the figure as a percentage of the total size of the group.

REASONS FOR USING PROJECT

Reason	Number (of 200)	Percent
Get leaflets	90	45
See member of staff	40	20
for class or activity	160	80
use cafe	100	50
just passing	20	10

Often there is a problem with some points of information not being recorded. For example, we might not know everyone's age. One approach is to add "not recorded/not known" to the list of categories. This was done in the first table in this section, and it is important to note this when you are doing your own rough tables and on the first occasion in the report when you give this information. Another approach is to exclude these cases and explain that this table shows the numbers and percentages of cases where the information was given. You then note, for example in a footnote below the table or in the text, how many were set aside. When you are doing more complicated analysis it is often simpler for your reader to do this. For example, if we had 300 people using the project, we would explain that the table showing the reasons for people using the project showed the proportion of those users who had told us their reasons for coming.

CATEGORIES

Many items, like age, are usually divided into categories. Use the bands which are most sensible in your circumstances. It does not have to be the ones noted here, even though this is a fairly standard division. For example, if you are providing a project for older people there would be little point in noting everyone as aged 60 and over. You would want to have categories of under 65-74, 75-84, 85 and over. Similarly, in Case Example 3 the project used the actual ages of young people who are all aged between 16-21.

For analysing information where there are no natural categories you have to create categories. Read through some of the forms or questionnaires or whatever and note key words or phrases which summarise points or views stated. If someone says something very similar to what is already on your list, put a tick beside it. Once you find you are mostly putting ticks rather than adding to the list, it is time to stop. Tidy up your list into a more logical order, for example bringing related points together. You can always add to the list as necessary as you go on to the next stage.

For individual cases or feedback forms etc, count these against the categories in the same way as we described for the factual categories like age. You can also list these out in the same way as for the multiple answer type of item. For example, our description of people's reasons for coming could have been drawn from people ticking pre-given categories on a form, or from their descriptions of why they came on a questionnaire.

Sometimes we are dealing with information about groups of people, for example when we have held a group discussion as in Case Example 11. The method is basically the same. However, here you cannot tie in the answers to individual people. However you can relate it to the group, or the numbers of groups, which made the response. The table below shows the way in which the project in this case example presented their findings from the user feedback.

FAMILY CENTRE: FEEDBACK FROM USERS' DISCUSSION GROUPS
PARENTS' COMMENTS

Responses concerning children	Mother and Toddler	Adult Educ	Residents' Group	Women's Group
Children enjoy the creche	*		*	
Learn new things	*	*		*
Able to play with other children	*		*	*
We can enjoy ourselves with the children	*			

Responses concerning themselves				
Feel less lonely	*			*
Group helps us grown in confidence	*	*	*	
Gives us a place to mix and have fun together	*	*	*	*

Responses concerning premises etc				
Location handy	*		*	*
Other parts of town need a similar place	*	*	*	*

CHILDREN'S COMMENTS

	5-8s after school	Youth Group	8-12 after school
Keeps us out of trouble			*
Making new friends	*	*	*
Fun with games, making things	*		*
Its safe – never any trouble		*	
You can talk to staff about problems, worries	*	*	*

5

Further Advice and Reading List

This handbook will not be able to answer every query you will have about monitoring and evaluation. It is also likely that by tackling monitoring and evaluation of your project or organisation you will come across other matters where you feel some assistance or advice would be useful.

At the time the research study on which this handbook is based was getting started there were few publications on monitoring and evaluation covering the circumstances of smaller voluntary organisations. Since then, more books and training materials have been published. Intermediary and training bodies have also published materials which address the needs of their particular member organisations but also have wider relevance. It may be a good idea to check what other material is available from the local authorities and other organisations with which you are in contact.

CHARITIES EVALUATION SERVICES

CES provides training, information, consultancy and advice on all aspects of monitoring and evaluation by voluntary organisations. It places particular emphasis on working alongside voluntary organisations and training people in self-evaluation skills. CES also provides advice and consultancy on monitoring and evaluation to funders. Planned developments include an extended resource bank of literature and training materials and a series of practical publications.

CES is a national organisation. There are presently 4 regional offices and more are planned. CES can be reached at:

> One Motley Avenue
> Christina Street
> LONDON
> EC2A 4SU

VOLUNTARY SECTOR INTERMEDIARY BODIES

The National Council of Voluntary Organisations and the equivalent bodies in Scotland, Wales and Northern Ireland are an important source of information.

They provide advice and information for membership organisations, newsletters and publications on a range of matters – including good management, planning and monitoring evaluation – and run training courses on a wide variety of topics. Some local intermediary bodies also have special activities of this sort.

In addition, intermediary bodies like Age Concern and Age Concern Scotland deal with the needs of local voluntary, statutory and other organisations concerned with the needs of particular groups of people. They may have material on planning and monitoring and evaluatary services which is also relevant to projects working with other groups of people.

FUNDERS

Many Trusts, Local Authorities, Health Boards and Government Departments provide information and advice for the voluntary organisations which they fund. Some also provide training courses and a few will provide or arrange one-off advice, for example on a consultancy basis.

ACADEMICS, CONSULTANTS ETC

An increasing number of people will provide advice or carry out monitoring and evaluation for voluntary organisations. In many cases this will be for payment – the levels vary widely. It may also be possible to get help through a student placement (for example, for people on community education, social work and similar courses) or a special course for staff wishing to evaluate an aspect of their service in greater depth, such as that supported by the Joseph Rowntree Foundation at the Social Work Research Centre, University of Stirling.

PUBLICATIONS ON PLANNING, SETTING AIMS AND TARGETS AND GENERAL MANAGEMENT

Barnes, Marion and Wistow, Gerald: Various papers and reports from the Birmingham Community Care Special Action Project; Nuffield Institute for Health Services, Leeds

James, Ann: Committed to Quality: Quality assurance in Social Services Departments; HMSO, 1992.

Pfeffer, Naomi and Coote, Anna: Is Quality good for you? Institute of Public Policy Research, 1991.

Shearer, Ann: Who Calls the Shots? Public services and how they serve the people who use them: Kings Fund Centre, 1992.

Whittaker, Andrea et al: Service Evaluation by People with Learning Difficulties; Kings Fund Centre, 1991. (Report from the Putting People First Project)

Wilson, Judy: Getting Started, Keeping Going; Longman, 1987.

PUBLICATIONS ON MONITORING AND EVALUATION

Ball, Mog: Evaluation in the Voluntary Sector; Forbes Trust, 1988.

Connor, Anne: Tell Them All About It; Age Concern Scotland, 1991.

Feek, Warren: Working Effectively – a guide to evaluation techniques; Bedford Square Press, 1988.

Hedley, Rodney: Measuring Success – a guide for voluntary and community groups; Advance.

Turner, Lesley and Willis, Elaine: Measuring-up – guidelines in the self-evaluation of voluntary projects; The Volunteer Centre.

Evaluation by Voluntary Organisations: Summary

BACKGROUND AND POLICY CONTEXT

This research study examined the potential for reliable monitoring and evaluation by voluntary organisations providing direct social care services of their own activities.

Monitoring: the regular checking of progress against a plan through routine, systematic collection of information.

Evaluation: judging the merit of an activity or plan by measuring it against specific criteria.

The study also developed practical methods to gather and analyse information which voluntary organisations can use. These are contained in a separate publication.

The study was carried out for Social Work Services Group of The Scottish Office to inform policy development and assist the implementation of policy and practice initiatives. These included:

- promoting the voluntary sector and the growth of volunteering;

- promoting choices to service users in the form of services and the way these are delivered;

- achieving greater effectiveness and efficiency in the use of resources, including public sector provision and financial support to the voluntary sector;

- extending services providing care in the community for people who are elderly, ill or have physical or mental disabilities; and

- increased emphasis on evaluation of policies initiated by Government departments.

Voluntary organisations are now expected to monitor and evaluate their activities in order to assist their own planning and ensure they are providing good quality services to users. They also need to provide feedback to the people and agencies, such as central and local government departments, which fund or have other interests in their activities. Existing monitoring and evaluation approaches were found to have limited impact in improving standards within voluntary organisations. The self-evaluation model which this study tested was devised to help bridge this gap. It complemented a range of other initiatives taken by Government departments aimed at improving aspects of management within the voluntary sector.

The research study set out to:

- identify the skills, resources and structures which voluntary organisations need in order to monitor and evaluate their own performance against agreed objectives;

- identify the types of information other organisations, such as funders, need to carry out their assessment of voluntary groups' performance;

- develop and test research-based monitoring and evaluation methods with some voluntary organisations in order to create a model which can then be used by other voluntary groups;

- assess the impact of this approach on the voluntary organisations' own performance; and

- assess the benefits to other agencies.

RESEARCH DESIGN

Fieldwork was carried out with 26 projects. These came from two main areas: Children and Families projects, provided by a major child care organisation (NCH Scotland) and day care centres for frail elderly people (identified through Age Concern Scotland). Between them these projects covered the range of characteristics relevant to information collection and evaluation: the size, type and circumstances of the voluntary organisation; the range of activities undertaken; complexity of information needs; and the state of existing record-keeping.

Fieldwork was completed over two years between November 1989 and December 1991. There were 6 main stages which overlapped with each other to some extent:

1. identification of relevant characteristics of projects;

2. identifying the information needs and developing methods to deal with these for the first set of fieldwork projects;

3. on-going contact with these projects to maintain information systems, identify emerging problems and further refine the methods;

4. introduce information systems to the remaining set of fieldwork projects;

5. check out the usefulness of systems being devised with other voluntary organisations, funders and referrers;

6. conduct a survey of local authority and health board funders' current and expected information requirements, particularly in light of the new community care arrangements.

EXPERIENCE OF PROJECTS PARTICIPATING IN FIELDWORK

The participating projects covered the range of stages of organisational development:

- those which were introducing monitoring and evaluation arrangements to a new project (5 projects);
- well-established services which were adding new or additional monitoring and evaluation arrangements (11 projects); and
- established projects which were coming up to a review or to the end of existing funding arrangements (9 projects).

One project was at the planning stage and the fieldwork was used to undertake a feasibility study.

The bulk of effort in planning and carrying out the monitoring and evaluation work fell on the co-ordinators and to a lesser extent other project staff. Key managers were involved in planning the work in half the cases and in carrying out the monitoring and evaluation in less than a third, although managers often gave other forms of support which greatly assisted the work. Other people such as committee members, users and representatives of funders or referrers were involved in the monitoring and evaluation work for only a handful of projects.

ISSUES TACKLED

The package of specific issues addressed and types of information gathering used was unique to each project, reflecting their circumstances, needs, information systems already in place and resources. However, the types of information problems and methods used to meet these were similar, even across projects working with different types of users and/or offering very different types of services. Six broad types of monitoring and evaluation work were identified:

- establishing the scale and pattern of use made of the service (19 of 26 projects);

- identifying outcomes of the service for the direct users, other people such as carers or parents and for other service providers (13 projects);

- feedback from users through surveys, interviews and other methods (14 projects);

- feedback from staff in other agencies (4 projects);

- organisational issues such as how staff spent their time and feedback from volunteers (4 projects); and

- feasibility studies for a potential new project or development of existing services (3 cases).

Each group of projects at different stages of development drew on the range of types of monitoring and evaluation work, but did so to varying extents and used this in different ways.

PROGRESS MADE

By the time the fieldwork for the study ended, 17 projects had completed the package of monitoring and evaluation tasks which they had set for themselves. Work was still continuing in 3 projects. In 6 cases the project had decided to stop with what they had completed, although they had the option of going back to this at a later stage.

Twenty-two projects gathered information for a specific exercise, such as a survey of users' views. Longer-term monitoring arrangements were introduced and have become well established for 14 projects; most of the remaining 12 projects already had good record-keeping systems. A systematic evaluation based on the data gathered occurred in 16 of the 26 projects. Some kind of formal report on the exercise was prepared by 14 projects, although many of the remaining 12 projects drew on the material for internal purposes or used it in less formal ways.

As might be expected, projects undertaking monitoring and evaluation work at different stages of their own development used this in different ways. For example, all 5 projects at the early stage of their development established ongoing monitoring systems but only one undertook an evaluation of its work so far. In contrast, 8 of the 9 projects expecting a review carried out their own evaluation but only 3 of these addressed the issue of ongoing monitoring.

There was no clear relationship between the range and complexity of monitoring and evaluation tasks attempted by projects and whether or not they completed this within their target timescale. The actual time taken for projects to do the work has ranged from 2 months to 15 months, reflecting a range of circumstances such as workload or staff levels as well as the type of monitoring and evaluation work tackled. From the experience of this fieldwork it seems that between 6 and 8 months is a reasonable target for most types of monitoring and evaluation work of the level attempted in this study. Almost all projects can expect to complete this within one year unless several difficulties arise.

FACTORS INFLUENCING PROGRESS

The study examined factors which could enhance or undermine projects' progress in completing monitoring and evaluation work. These fell into three broad areas:

- factors internal to the project, such as availability of secretarial support, sick leave and other staff shortages etc;

- aspects of the project's relationship with the outside world, such as lack of clarity about the criteria against which a funder would assess the project's success; and

- features of the monitoring and evaluation work itself, such as tackling areas which were technically very complex or which required resources such as computer packages for analysis of data which were not available to the project.

The most significant factor in whether or not the projects completed the work was the level of management support. All projects which completed the work on time had substantial or routine management input. For those projects which had only a minimal management input, no work was finished on time and only two of these seven projects completed the monitoring and evaluation tasks which they had set.

Other factors which appeared to have a major impact on whether or not projects were able to complete work at all or on time were:

- significant staff illnesses or vacancies, especially of the coordinator;

- the timing and use which other people will make of the results, especially in reviews of project funding: this was therefore linked to the stage of project development; and

- project staff's level of confidence in whether any use would be made of the findings.

Other factors were clarified which did not have a major impact on whether or not the work was completed and on time but still had an impact in making the task easier or more difficult. These included:

- the level of secretarial support;

- the workload faced by the project;
- the clarity of the project's aims and objectives and of the funders' criteria; and
- the need to integrate with other information systems set by other agencies.

Some form of complication can be expected to be the norm: only one project came across no complications or delays and the evaluation work ran as expected.

These factors interacted with each other to compound or balance out the impact on the progress of the monitoring and evaluation work. For example, among projects which had routine or substantial management input, those which were not finished or were late were noticeably more likely to have experienced substantial staff or volunteer vacancies or levels of sick leave and relatively more often had heavy demands on the project than had those which completed the work on time. The seven projects where the evaluation tasks were finished late or only partially done and had minimal management input included all three examples of projects which had no agreed aims and objectives or which had not checked the funders' criteria for the project, while five of these expected no use to be made of the results, mostly because staff felt managers had no interest.

The circumstances of some projects did make it especially difficult to carry out particular tasks such as monitor the level of certain activities or gain feedback from users. Although methods were found to tackle most of these problems, for these projects the evaluation work tended to take longer to complete, be more disruptive for the project or place other additional demands on the project. In a few cases it had to be accepted that it was beyond the resources and skills of the project to address a particular issue at that time.

HOW THE INFORMATION WAS USED

Impact on Voluntary Organisations
Most of the participating voluntary projects (22 of 26) found the monitoring and evaluation input helped to improve direct service to users and assisted their contacts with other agencies. The main advantages identified by projects were:

- easier and better quality feedback to managers and outside interests such as local authorities and The Scottish Office;
- meeting the requirements of different funders/agencies with no or minimal duplication;
- feeding the information into internal planning, such as a major review or on-going feedback from users;

- helping the project address the issue of change, such as helping people accept the need for change or enabling the project to resist specific changes suggested from elsewhere; and

- drawing on material for training.

These monitoring and evaluation exercises were not specifically planned to make savings or efficiencies: however, 12 projects identified resource benefits as a consequence. The most common circumstance was where a simplified information system saved staff time which had previously been spent on administration.

Four projects did not find the monitoring and evaluation work helpful. All four were from the group of projects which never expected much use to be made of the information gathered and in each case did not carry through to the evaluation stage.

An important issue for projects was the time taken to gather and analyse the information, which they set against the benefits gained and other demands on them. However, the amount of time taken was not a significant factor in projects' assessment of overall usefulness.

Benefits to projects were also identified by other people such as managers, other staff with overall responsibilities and local authority staff who worked with projects. These included:

- greater clarity and better quality in the way the project presented itself in annual reports, funding applications and forward plans;

- higher levels of motivation among project staff; and

- project staff becoming more confident in dealing with referrers and other people outside the project.

As a result, the projects put more demands on their managers and other agencies. Some of the people concerned found this positive but others resented the additional demands, typically when the monitoring and evaluation highlighted pre-existing problems which were thought to have no solution.

Projects' Feedback to Funders and Referrers
Almost all projects (24 of 26) fed information from the monitoring and evaluation work back to people who made referrals to the project and/or staff who were responsible for funding the service. This feedback was mostly planned and done through a range of informal and formal means. However, not all the reports reached all those who had an interest in the project. The information reached the staff with responsibility for referrals of individual users in virtually

all cases, reached staff with responsibility for administering or monitoring funding in two-thirds of cases, but reached staff with overall policy responsibility for this client group or type of service in only one-third of cases.

A third of projects received no response other than an acknowledgement, which the project staff found very disappointing. The responses made by the other two-thirds of agencies were mostly described by projects as encouraging: these were positive comments about the project's activities and the report itself and/or more critical questions about the quality or focus of the service, which often led to a useful discussion about future development. Eight projects also received more discouraging responses, including inappropriate or inaccurate assumptions about the level or type of service, the application of inappropriate criteria and inappropriate comparisons with other services. This feedback in turn led to various practical consequences for the projects, including an improvement in the funding level or security of four projects. Some projects had experience of positive responses posing difficulties when local staff in the statutory service resented what appeared to be an indirect criticism of them by their managers.

The views of the people receiving these reports on the usefulness and benefits to the funding or referring agency is known in 15 cases. Generally, feedback was considered an improvement on what was usually submitted through annual reports. Staff in central administrative or policy sections made greater use of the reports they received than their colleagues in local settings with responsibility for direct care. There were some instances of local authority staff describing the reports as very useful when the project itself felt that no-one had paid any attention to the document.

Benefits to Users

The study also identified specific benefits to the users of projects' services as a consequence of the monitoring and evaluation systems which were introduced. These benefits were confirmed in general terms by other professionals involved with that user group. These benefits were mostly as a consequence of better case management or case review systems, similar to those which will be needed for the care management arrangements under the community care provisions, while some projects were able to increase the number of people receiving a service and/or improve the input to existing users.

BLOCKS TO FURTHER IMPACT

It would have been possible for the projects themselves and other people with an interest in their activities to have made better use of the information gathered.

The majority (three-quarters) of projects made good use of the material gathered and may exploit it further in the longer-term. For the remaining projects, the most common situation where the work had limited impact was in not using feedback for internal planning because staff and/or managers were not looking for positive improvements or because they doubted if any changes could be put into effect. The other circumstance where projects made limited use of their monitoring and evaluations was in not linking this into annual and other applications for funding.

Limitations in the way funding and referring agencies used the information were more common. These circumstances included reports and feedback not reaching the right people, coming at the wrong time or not addressing the recipient organisation's concerns, and projects being less open about matters on which they expected a critical response, often on the basis of previous experiences.

The experience of other projects within the fieldwork has shown how these blocks can be avoided or minimised.

REQUIREMENTS OF FUNDERS

Arrangements for Fieldwork Projects
The way in which funding and referring agencies are organised and the information required from voluntary organisations changed over the period of this research study and is expected to be reviewed further over the coming year or so as the effects of the Review of Government Funding of the Voluntary Sector and the Care in the Community arrangements become clearer.

There was often a gap between the types of information needed by people making assessments about projects for the purposes of referring clients or for continued financial support, which emphasised qualitative aspects of the service and management arrangements, and the information which projects were asked to provide under the terms of the financial arrangements, which focused on the financial aspects and the scale of service delivery.

The great majority of projects in this fieldwork were receiving funding from several sources, which further complicated the types of feedback which they had to make to different agencies: this is known to be typical of many direct service voluntary projects providing social care.

Types of Financial Support
In terms of the type of financial input and associated accountability, overall these projects were, or had recently been, moving along a spectrum to more formal

types of financial support. Most had moved from a *contribution*, with minimal expectations on each side, to *grants* for identified purposes and levels of activity. None of the projects was involved in a more formal service agreement or similar type of contract.

The survey of local authority Social Work and Education Departments and Health Boards showed that, overall, grants and service agreements will become the usual forms of financial support, with contribution-type arrangements and formal contracts being used in very specific, exceptional circumstances, although the balance used by individual funders may differ. Several authorities were making changes to the conditions of grant and their internal arrangements in response to the Community Care requirements which were expected to apply to all voluntary organisations, irrespective of the user group involved.

Funders' Administrative Arrangements
Funders had developed various ways of handling the selection, payment and monitoring of financial support to voluntary organisations in response to a wide range of policies and circumstances. These were grouped into four broad types, each of which has certain advantages and disadvantages for the funder itself and/or recipient voluntary organisations. Under the new arrangements the most frequent model will be a single section or occasionally a single person being responsible for all funding matters – including liaison with other funders – irrespective of the type of grant, service or user group.

In terms of communication within and between funders, especially between those planning for the care of individuals or groups of users and those responsible for the financial input to the voluntary organisation, again four general models were identified. In this, there was a greater spread of approaches between the Social Work Departments, while Health Boards were divided between two models and Education Departments used a more consistent approach. Those authorities which had a split between the planning/monitoring of services and the financial aspects were planning to introduce arrangements to ensure easier links between these areas of responsibility. However, plans for increased communication between authorities and other funders focused on overall policy matters and allocation of lead responsibility, rather than more detailed arrangements for specific voluntary projects.

Implications for Voluntary Organisations
A list of information points which are likely to be needed for all or most projects was identified. The voluntary organisations in this fieldwork for the most part agreed with the statutory agencies about the types of information which are

needed for any full, proper assessment of the effectiveness and efficiency of projects. However, in most instances, funders' current arrangements did not request these, although revised conditions of financial awards may become increasingly specific.

ASSESSMENT AND CONCLUSIONS

Achievements of Study and Self-Evaluation Approach
The study succeeded in identifying the information needs of direct service voluntary organisations, especially in establishing the quality of services to users. It also succeeded in developing methods to tackle those needs.

The experience of the study demonstrated the way performance review tasks and skills interact with other aspects of management and planning. The study confirmed that a flexible approach to information gathering and review is required.

When information requirements were met, the voluntary projects benefited in their day-to-day operation, in longer-term planning and development and in the quality and scale of service given to users. These in turn sometimes put pressure on project managers and other agencies, for example when they were unable or unwilling to meet the raised expectations.

Good quality monitoring and evaluation by voluntary organisations could also contribute to positive relationships with other agencies such as funders, but could also highlight pre-existing tensions. Other people generally considered that the quality of information from the participating projects had improved and was helpful, although this was not always made clear to funded projects.

Most projects had sufficient skills and resources to carry out and make constructive use of the monitoring and evaluation tasks within this approach. Essential factors in this were:

- sufficient time, people able to carry out the tasks, management support and practical resources;
- the necessary monitoring and evaluation skills, including an ability to interpret and present findings: outside help is especially useful here;
- structures which enable the findings and any associated changes to be put into effect; and
- a willingness to listen and consider scope for improvement and change.

The impact of the monitoring and evaluation work was also dependent on the responses of the funders and referrers. Specific steps to improve the situation, already taken by some local authorities and other bodies, are:

- better communication with voluntary organisations;
- better internal communication within authorities; and
- being realistic about what information projects can provide.

Limitations of Self-Evaluation Approach
This self-evaluation approach has limitations which need to be kept in mind.

- Its potential application to several important areas of voluntary sector activity has not been tested – financial monitoring, management effectiveness and the role of intermediary organisations. The self-evaluation approach may usefully complement other performance review methods for these topics but further development will be needed.
- The success of the approach in completion of the monitoring and evaluation work and resultant improvements to services will be limited when the management of the project is poor. Also this approach will not in itself contribute to improved management.
- This approach is built around the needs of the projects. It takes account of many information needs of other agencies but cannot be expected to tackle all of these. Funders will still need to make their own arrangements for monitoring and evaluation against their criteria, although this should be easier and quicker when self-evaluation arrangements are in place.

SUMMING UP

Overall, the study has demonstrated that monitoring and evaluation by direct service voluntary projects can be done to a sufficient standard for their own and other agencies' quality assurance and planning needs. To do this, several factors must first be in place.

- The organisation must be clear what it is monitoring and evaluating its achievements against.
- The project and other people must be realistic about what can be done in those circumstances.
- The project must have good management support.
- The people concerned, especially the project staff, must believe that this is worthwhile and that there is scope for positive changes if necessary.

Printed in Scotland for HMSO by HMSO Press
Dd 287529 C30 3/93 (206275)